DAVID W. NELSON
12, Clos Nollet
91-ATHIS-MONS FRANCE

YES, BUT...

YES, BUT...

**REASONABLE QUESTIONS
ABOUT LIVING FAITH**

Roger T. Forster M.A.
and
V. Paul Marston M.Sc.

VICTORY PRESS
Eastbourne

First Published 1971
© R.T.Forster and V.P.Marston 1971
Reprinted 1971

Printed in Great Britain for
Evangelical Publishers Limited
Lottbridge Drove, Eastbourne, Sussex
by Compton Printing Limited
London and Aylesbury

INTRODUCTION

YES, the cross which became the symbol of Christianity appears in many places in modern society. **BUT** is the real message of Christianity relevant for today? Can anyone believe in God in this age of science? Could a God of love permit suffering? Doesn't religion restrict man's liberty?

This book is written for those who, like the authors, believe that these questions should be asked. One of the authors graduated from Cambridge and has since spent some time in running an extended family unit for the maladjusted, as well as conducting pastoral work and evangelism in this country and throughout Europe; the other recently completed his studies at the London School of Economics and is now a lecturer in statistical methods and operational research at a London business school. They are united in a belief that the Christian faith is both true and reasonable, and that answers exist to reasonable questions about it. In this book they outline replies to twenty-nine such questions which they have often been asked by thinking people, especially students. The answers are not presented as though complete and definitive, but in the hope that some of the ideas may stimulate other people as they develop their own solutions. The sections are necessarily short and condensed, so the carefully selected further reading guides are an important part of the book, enabling the reader to pursue some of the subjects in greater detail.

CONTENTS

1. Why should I bother about religion?

2. When there are so many religions why consider Christianity in particular?

3. Couldn't this Jesus have been an eccentric or even a legendary figure?

4. How reliable are these records we have about Jesus?

5. Is there any mention of Jesus outside the Bible?

6. How can we believe such fantastic accounts of miracles and so on, in this modern age of science?

7. Since we do not see miracles today, couldn't it be that people used to be more simple?

8. Miracles aside—doesn't the Bible contain unscientific explanations of natural processes?

9. Doesn't the Bible ascribe psychological illness to demons?

10. Does this mean that you take the Bible literally— Adam and Eve and all?

11. Even if the Bible is not wrong on specific points, is not the whole view of the world according to science a different one?

12. Christians often seem to me to argue in circles!

13. Where did God come from, and what did he do before the universe began?

14. Is it rational to believe that a God of love could create a universe as full of pain as ours?

15. What about disease, is that a result of sin?

CONTENTS

What of the animal world, where there is so much killing and suffering?	16
What would you say to one who is actually suffering?	17
Doesn't the Bible show a moral inconsistency between the God of wrath in the Old Testament and the God of love in the New?	18
Doesn't the Bible show an unhealthy preoccupation with blood and sacrifice?	19
If God loves everyone then what happens to those who have never heard?	20
Then why bother to preach, if all religions lead to God?	21
Even if everyone seems to have some opportunity to believe, what is the point of torturing unbelievers for ever?	22
Can't I be good without being a Christian?	23
But religious people always seem to be concerned with such silly little things!	24
Then you don't think that Christianity is narrow and restrictive?	25
But aren't Christians afraid of sex experience?	26
What exactly does it mean to be a Christian?	27
You Christians always quote the Bible, do I have to believe it all to become a Christian?	28
What would I do to become a Christian?	29
Foreword to Professing Existentialists.	

WHY SHOULD I BOTHER ABOUT RELIGION?

The psychiatrist Dr Paul Tournier writes: 'Let us be the first to discover what modern man is seeking. He is thirsting for God. . . . Everybody today is searching for an answer to those problems to which science pays no attention, the problem of their destiny, the mystery of evil, the question of death.'[1] The science and arts of the late nineteenth century were largely dominated by an atmosphere of optimism. That optimism has now generally evaporated. One leading popular exponent of this movement was the agnostic H.G.Wells. By the time of his death in 1946 he was overwhelmed by disillusionment and despair. Another famous agnostic and prophet of heaven on earth was Professor C.E.M.Joad. In later life he too became disillusioned, but made a further discovery and wrote: 'The rationalist-optimist philosophy by the light of which I had done my best to live came to seem intolerably trivial and superficial . . . unable to withstand the bleaker winds of the twentieth century. I abandoned it and found myself a Christian.' Malcolm Muggeridge tells us that he too was 'brought up to be an ardent believer in utopianism.'[2] Yet in 1968 he can write: 'As far as I am concerned it is Christ or nothing.'[3] Whatever we think about these outstanding examples, it is clear that utopianism has largely collapsed. In the wake of this there is today a moral and spiritual vacuum, especially in the rising generations. In making this general observation we are not joining the ranks of those who, down the centuries, have proclaimed that their own younger generation must surely be the worst; for it is not a moral degeneracy of which we speak. It is rather the loss of *any* sort of vision (Christian or otherwise) able to give a meaning to life. Nearly all artists and novelists seem to be aware of this, even if the personal philosophies of some of them are still optimistic. How could they not realize it when they consider the work of Gauguin or Kafka, Beckett or Sartre, or the whole movement in language since Rimbaud? The music of John Cage and the painting of Jackson Pollock may be extreme examples because they are consciously expressing the meaninglessness of life. Nevertheless, most of those involved in modern artistic expression are aware that there *is* a problem in finding or expressing a meaning to life. Through the media of folk and pop music this meaninglessness has also been conveyed to a more general public. It has been demonstrated by artists such as Roy Harper, David Ackles, and others including at some stage the more popular Beatles and Paul Simon.

Many people may not yet realize what has happened. Some of us may have successfully filled up our own lives, and avoid thinking about questions like: has life a meaning? Others of us may have realized that what we live for does not bring fulfilment, but cling to it in fear of nothingness. Muggeridge writes: 'I never met a man made happy by worldly success or sensual indulgence, still less by the stupefaction of drugs or alchohol. Yet we all, in one way or another, pursue these ends, as the advertiser well knows.'[4] To say that people cannot achieve some sort of happiness would be absurd. Having achieved it, however, we are always left with a vague feeling that somehow there ought to be more to life than merely this. Do our lives ultimately have no more meaning than a 'huge ugly joke, braying across the universe'?[5] We can repress this question. We try to fill our lives well enough to forget it. Yet, whatever our age or intellect, the problem remains.

Two major philosophers: Nietzsche in Germany and now Sartre in France, have understood well the connection between meaninglessness and the disappearance of God from our beliefs. Nietzsche could not stand the idea of God always watching him and loving him even in his evil; he determined, therefore, that God *had to die*![6] Man was then supposed to laugh in the face of the emptiness of the universe, and rise above it to become superman.[7] Nietzsche himself, however, was unable to do this; his mind snapped under the strain (we say this with compassion) and for the last years of his life he was insane.

Jean-Paul Sartre wrote in 1947: 'The existentialist finds

it extremely embarrassing that God does not exist, for there disappears with him all possibility of finding values in an intelligible heaven.'[8] Nevertheless, at that stage he still seemed basically optimistic that man could create meaning for himself. In 1964 he likens himself to a traveller without any meaning or vocation, and writes: 'Atheism is a cruel long-term business.'[9] Few people have faced the problem of meaninglessness in a universe without God as directly as have these two great philosophers, yet it is a problem which affects us all.

Christianity claims to give man a real meaning and purpose for the fullest development of his being in all its potentialities: mental, aesthetic and spiritual. It presents man as a creature made in the image of a personal God, and capable of receiving eternal life, becoming God's child through faith. In this way, man may find his place in the universe, beginning to live in God's way in His world. Christianity claims, moreover, to solve man's universal problem of death (which seems to deny any meaning to the individual) for in the historical resurrection of the man Jesus Christ, death has both been defeated and been shown to be defeated. Now all this may be mistaken, it may be a lie, it may be raising false hopes, it may be a wishful dream, but the one thing which it certainly is *not*, is irrelevant to contemporary man. If we are talking about the authentic message of Jesus, and not some anaemic version of Christianity, then it is certainly worth bothering to find out what it says and whether it is true.

Further Reading:

Unafraid To Be Ruth Etchells (I.V.P.)
A lecturer in English examines the problem of man's identity, as shown in contemporary literature.

Another King Malcolm Muggeridge
(St Andrew Press: now included in *Jesus Rediscovered*.)
The sermon preached by Mr Muggeridge at the time of his controversial resignation from the chancellorship of Edinburgh University.

The Dilemma of Modern Man W.Hurvey Woodson (S.T.L.)
A booklet dealing with the search for purpose in life.

The Mark of Cain S. Barton Babbage (Paternoster)
Dr Babbage suggests that Christ is the answer to the
problem of meaninglessness which is raised in literature.

Christian Counter Attack Arnold Lunn and Garth Lean
(Blandford)
The authors, an Anglican and a Catholic, make some
thoughtful points about problems in our society, and call
on Christians to proclaim their faith.

Notes for Section 1

1. *The Whole Person in a Broken World* p.149.

2. *Jesus Rediscovered* p.15.

3. From the *Another King* sermon originally published by
   St Andrew Press, later *Jesus Rediscovered* p.97.

4. *Jesus Rediscovered* p.96.

5. H.G. Wells.

6. See e.g. *Thus Spoke Zarathustra* in the words of the Ugliest Man.

7. See e.g. in Zarathustra's words to the Higher Men: 'He who sees
   the abyss, but with an eagle's eyes—he who *grasps* the abyss with
   an eagle's claws: *he* possesses courage.' We are, of course, aware
   of the difficulty of being certain of Nietzsche's exact meaning,
   caused by his comparatively unsystematic approach.

8. *Existentialism and Humanism* p.33.

9. This is in the last chapter of the first part of Sartre's
   autobiography: *Words*.

WHEN THERE ARE SO MANY RELIGIONS WHY CONSIDER CHRISTIANITY IN PARTICULAR?

2

When considering any religion or philosophy, we should first ask ourselves 'what is it that it claims to do?' Most philosophical systems are the conscious attempts of different men to reach up and discover the truth about our world. World religions are generally more intuitive in origin. Buddhism sprang from one man's answer to the problem of human suffering—the noble eightfold path. In the Hindu faith, one is seeking an experiential understanding of the oneness of God in everything, including pain and suffering. The more primitive animism (or spirit worship) which is common to many different peoples, involves man's attempts to placate unknown powers. From all such world systems Christianity stands out by claiming to be a revelation from a personal creator. The claim that God has communicated to man should, of itself, demand our attention, irrespective of the conclusions we reach.

Judaism and Islam are the other two world religions claiming to embody such a revelation from a personal God. No one could seriously consider Judaism without, logically at least, looking at Jesus' claim to be the Jewish Messiah. Islam's sacred book, the Koran, is short enough even for busy people to read, and in it Jesus is accepted as a prophet. Logically therefore, one should go back and study also what Jesus said.

Christainity is unlike *all* other religions in that it is based on the personal and unique claims of the historical figure Jesus of Nazareth. Two thousand years ago this man reportedly went about in Palestine doing miracles. He claimed to be able to forgive sins,[1] and he claimed to be the way, the truth and the life—in fact that he was the only way to God.[2] Although a strict monotheist, he accepted the worship of others on numerous occasions. Finally he said that he had come to die for the world, but would rise again from the dead[3] and so defeat death in a way no other religion had done.[4] He deliberately allowed himself to be captured, tried and crucified. If there is any truth at all in our records about him, then we must conclude either that he was insane or that he was in fact what he claimed to be. What we *cannot* conclude is that he was 'just a good man'. Would we really describe as good anyone else who made such fantastic claims for himself? Other men whom we regard as great and good invariably emphasize their own unworthiness. For example, St Francis once explained that God used him so much because there was nowhere a greater sinner or a more miserable creature than he. Either Jesus was good and what he claimed to be, or else, consciously or unconsciously, he was deceiving us. Yet the very enormity of his claims, together with the uniqueness of his person, should lead us to consider Christianity seriously.

Further Reading:

The Four Gospels
Anyone wanting to seriously consider Christianity should surely read the source books for the life of Christ, preferably in a modern translation.

Basic Christianity John R.W.Stott (I.V.P.)
A study of the person and life of Christ is followed by an attempt to relate his work to the need of mankind.

A Life of Christ Malcolm Muggeridge
(St Andrew Press, now also included in *Jesus Rediscovered*)
A B.B.C. colour film was made in Palestine of Mr Muggeridge talking about the gospel story and the uniqueness of Jesus. This is the text of his commentary.

Jesus the Messiah Alfred Edersheim (Longmans)
A biography by one of the great experts on the Jewish historical background to Christ.

Notes for Section 2

1. Mark 2.5; Luke 5.20.
2. John 14.6.
3. Matthew 16.21; 17.9,22; Luke 9.22; 17.25; 18.33.
4. See also Section 3.

COULDN'T THIS JESUS HAVE BEEN AN ECCENTRIC OR EVEN A LEGENDARY FIGURE?

3

We hope that anyone determined to maintain this view has at least read the four Gospels thoughtfully in adulthood. All too often such an opinion is based on vaguely remembered snippets of school Religious Instruction. If, after thoughtful study, one does decide that Jesus was insane, one is still left with certain things unexplained.

For instance, a number of people claimed to have seen him alive after he had been crucified and buried; and the four accounts which we have of this may be fitted together. There are even little touches of circumstantial evidence.[1] None of the explanations offered by sceptics of these accounts seem to us to be plausible. Could the appearances be explained as hallucinations? We must remember that Christ was sometimes seen by large groups of different types of people, all at the same time. He spoke to them and on one occasion ate something. The appearances occurred at all times of day, inside and outside, and continued for just forty days after which they stopped. All these facts militate against the suggestion that the resurrection appearances are to be explained as hallucinations or as psychic phenomena. Could it have been some kind of mistake? In this case the authorities could easily have suppressed what they regarded as a dangerous new teaching simply by producing the body. Its disappearance cannot be ascribed to ordinary grave-robbers, for they would hardly steal a body and leave the grave-clothes. If it was part of a plot by the disciples to hoodwink the world, why then did they run for cover when Jesus was arrested and yet six weeks later have the courage to defy the authorities? More seriously, are we to believe that their high moral teaching was based on a gigantic lie?

Can we suppose, too, that they stuck to this lie even though many were martyred for it? Dr Schonfield's recent attempt at explanation along these lines is even less reasonable.[2] He admits that Jesus was sincere. He accepts that Jesus believed both in himself and in the power of God. Yet he supposes him to have arranged a fraud which would be quite unnecessary if God were really powerful. It is a little surprising that a theory with so basic a flaw should come from a scholar who is undeniably eminent in his field.

Others have suggested that the Gospel records of Jesus are very much coloured by later legend, and that perhaps he never existed, or was only a teacher in the Dead Sea Sect. Such speculations cannot seriously be entertained, for third century legends about Jesus are indeed available for comparison with the Gospels. The latter differ, firstly, in their accurate picture of the situation of the first century, and secondly in the vivid way in which Jesus is portrayed against this background. One of our leading New Testament scholars writes: 'It is difficult enough for anyone, even a consummate master of imaginative writing, to create a picture of a deeply pure, good person moving about in an impure environment, without making him a prig or a prude or a "plaster saint". How comes it that, through all the Gospel traditions without exception, there comes a remarkably finely drawn portrait of an attractive young man moving freely about among women of all sorts, including the decidedly disreputable, without a trace of sentimentality, unnaturalness, or prudery, and yet, at every point, maintaining a simple integrity of character? Is this because the environment in which the traditions were preserved and through which they were transmitted were peculiarly favourable to such a portrait? On the contrary, it seems that they were rather hostile to it.'[3] Another example of this atmosphere of veracity surrounding the Jesus of the Gospels, is his capacity for doing what is at first sight unexpected and yet what, when one thinks about it, seems inevitable[4] No legends breathe the atmosphere of reality displayed by the resurrection accounts in which a woman with a dubious past is the first to see Jesus, the insignificant and otherwise unknown Cleopas receives a front place, and the Lord's first meeting with Peter is never even described.

The New Testament records present a Jesus who seems

neither eccentric nor legendary. On the contrary, he is both consistently and realistically portrayed.

Further Reading:

Christianity; the Witness of History J.N.D.Anderson (Tyndale)
The Evidence for the Resurrection J.N.D.Anderson (I.V.P.)
A London University Law Professor sifts the various evidences about Jesus and his resurrection.

Who Moved the Stone? Frank Morison (Faber)
The author planned to write a book to disprove the resurrection. As he studied the evidence he was driven to conclude that it did occur, and instead wrote this book.

The Davidson Affair Stuart Jackman (Faber)
A short, skilfully conceived and executed documentary fiction-fantasy of Christ's martyrdom and resurrection, viewed through the techniques of modern television.' *The Sunday Times*.

Notes for Section 3

1. For example: Unlike the other Gospel writers, John does not mention the women who accompanied Mary until she turned back at the edge of the garden. Nevertheless, in John 20.2 she uses the plural: 'and *we* do not know where they have laid him.'

2. *The Passover Plot* by H.J.Schonfield (first published 1965).

3. *The Phenomenon of the New Testament* C.F.D.Moule

4. e.g. Mark 12.17; John 8.7; Mark 9.36.

HOW RELIABLE ARE THESE RECORDS WE HAVE ABOUT JESUS?

4

In various museums there are preserved the very early Greek documents from which our New Testament has been translated. In all there are about 4,500 Greek texts, some of which are as early as the first few centuries. We have, for example, the Rylands fragment of John from the early second century, the Bodmer ii portions of the same Gospel from the early third century, and the almost complete New Testament in the Chester Beatty papyri of the same date. From the fourth century we have the beautiful and complete Siniaticus and Vaticanus codices, and from the fifth century the codex Alexandrinus and others. The New Testament manuscripts are older, and more numerous, than almost any classical work[1] and the differences between them are nearly always trivial.

The text of these manuscripts, for example of the Gospels and the Acts, presents a picture of the first century world which fits well with the other information we have concerning it. In the book of the Acts, Luke gives much historical detail which, to any age after his own and before the advent of modern archaeology, would have been inaccessible. How could he discover the 15 different titles of Roman governors given accurately in his writing[2] unless he were at least a contemporary? The great archaeologist Sir William Ramsey first seriously considered Christianity after noting that in the Acts Luke supplied a geographical detail that a later age would not have known. Such evidences may convince us, as they convinced him, that the New Testament documents are indeed genuine and reliable.[3]

Further Reading:

The New Testament Documents, Are They Reliable?
F.F.Bruce (I.V.P.)
The Rylands professor of Biblical Criticism at Manchester University considers this important question.

Archaeology of the New Testament R.K.Harrison (Hodder)
Professor Harrison writes with the general reader in mind, but with notes and bibliography for the specialist.

Ring of Truth J.B.Phillips (Hodder)
A famous translator testifies to his own experience of close textual examination of the Bible.

Notes for Section 4

1. The text of Caesar's *Gallic Wars* for example, is based on a single ninth century manuscript.

2. e.g. Proconsuls, Asiarchs, Praetors, Lictors, Politarchs, First-Man, Tetrarch, and Procurator.

3. Another archaeologist, Dr W.F.Albright, who is perhaps the greatest orientalist in the world today, wrote in 1958: 'The sensational finds among the Dead Sea Scrolls since 1948 bring an even more complete revaluation of what has passed for historic-literary criticism of the New Testament. At long last we possess original Hebrew and Aramaic religious books from the century and a half before the Crucifixion... There is no longer any concrete evidence for dating a single New Testament book after the seventies or eighties of the first century A.D... To sum up, we can now again treat the Bible from beginning to end as an authentic document of religious history.' (*The Christian Century*, November 1958).

IS THERE ANY MENTION OF JESUS OUTSIDE THE BIBLE?

One could not expect the records of Rome to pay great attention to a crucified Jewish criminal in an obscure province, but some early writings do allude to him. It is possible that the excuse made by the authorities for the disappearance of Jesus' body¹ filtered back to the Roman bureaucracy and was the cause of a marble inscription in Nazareth dating back to the reign of Claudius (A.D. 41-54) threatening the death penalty for the removal of bodies from tombs. It was also during Claudius' reign that the Jews were expelled from Rome because of 'riots at the instigation of Chrestos', perhaps a misunderstanding of disturbances in the Jewish quarter when Christ was preached. In this same reign, and a mere 20 years after the crucifixion, people were being buried with inscriptions mentioning Jesus on their tombs. Two were discovered in 1945 by Professor Sukenik inscribed 'Jesus help' and, it seems, 'Jesus, let him arise'. The Roman historian Tacitus (c A.D. 55-118) mentions that the Christians derive their name from Christ, who was executed under the procurator Pontius Pilate (*Annals* 15.44). Various other Romans mention early

Christianity, but the best witness to Jesus comes from
Josephus, a non-Christian Jewish historian (c A.D. 37-95)
Professor Bruce (above) analyses various passages in
Josephus' writings, including *Antiquities* xviii 3.3, where
Jesus' miracles and his reported resurrection are mentioned.[2]
Lastly we should mention the early inscriptions by
Christians themselves in the city of Pompeii, which was
covered by volcanic action in A.D. 79.

Further Reading:

Runaway World Michael Green (I.V.P.)
'Is it the believer or the unbeliever who is running away
from reality?' asks the author. The book includes much
material useful to this and the previous section.

Beyond the Gospels R.Dunkerly (Pelican)
An account, by a London University professor, of
information about Jesus found outside the Gospels.

Notes for Section 5

1. Matthew 28.11-15.
2. *The New Testament Documents, Are They Reliable?* p.102-112.

HOW CAN WE BELIEVE SUCH FANTASTIC ACCOUNTS OF MIRACLES AND SO ON, IN THIS MODERN AGE OF SCIENCE?

6 The word miracle is commonly used in two different ways:
(1) It is used to describe a natural but often unusual event
which occurs at the very time it is required, perhaps as an
answer to prayer. A good example is when Jesus commanded
the storm to cease, and it did.[1] There was nothing in the
cessation of the storm which differed from the normal

processes studied in science—it could have been described as coincidence. The miracle was in that the event came precisely when it did. A similar example was the catch of fish, made suddenly at a time when no fisherman would have expected it.[2] A third example was the feeding of Elijah by ravens.[3] Such events are, to say the least, unusual, but there is nothing in them which is contrary to our laws of science.

It may be that, as science and knowledge progress, we will discover many more of the Bible miracles to be examples of this. We might, for example, discover natural explanations for the first nine plagues sent on Pharoah.[4] Should this prove to be the case then it will in no way detract from a belief in the accuracy of the Bible. The Bible writers did not have any firm concept of 'scientific laws'. They were not, therefore, interested in distinguishing between a miracle in which something occurred contrary to such laws, and one which could conceivably be ascribed to coincidence. Their interest was, quite rightly, solely in the fact that *God* had caused it for some purpose.

(2) The word miracle is sometimes used to describe an event which we are unable to explain in terms of our laws of science. Two examples of this are the virgin birth of Jesus and the feeding of the five thousand. Such events can-cannot be explained at all in terms of the normal physical cause-effect of our scientific laws, and so have been a problem to some people.

In considering this we must think carefully, not only about what exactly the Bible says, but also about what our so-called scientific laws really are. It is unfortunate that the popular use of emotive words like *break* and *laws* has misled many people, especially non-scientists. 'Scientific laws' are essentially generalizations about causes and effects, which we ourselves fit to human observations. To many people the word *law* may carry undertones of necessity, compulsion and universality, which are quite outside its valid use in this context. We talk of *breaking* or *discovering* laws, as though they had some independent objective existence, and could themselves compel events. Take, for example, the law of gravity. It was observed that certain events (an apple falls) usually follow certain causes (the release of an apple near to the earth's surface). From observation of such phenomena a law of gravity was formulated. The law of gravity, however, neither dictates that events should always follow this pattern, nor does it explain them.[5]

A *scientific law* is at most a generalization about what is normally observed to occur; and a description of normal occurrences could never dictate to us whether or not there could be abnormal ones. To use a crude analogy: to say that man is a biped is not to deny humanity to someone who has a wooden leg! Now if the Bible had reported that virgin births were an everyday event, then we might check this by scientific observation. If it says that one such birth occurred as a unique event in history then no generalization in science could be relevant. One cannot disprove a claim that two thousand years ago an unusual, if not unique, event took place, by showing that such events do not happen every day.

A possible explanation of why some people in the past seem to have found a problem in this area is that scientific laws were wrongly supposed to contain total explanations. Let us use as an illustration Boyle's law: *The volume of a given mass of gas is inversely proportional to the pressure upon it if the temperature remains constant.* This law describes what normally happens, but it does not say (i) *why* it happens or (ii) why it should *always* happen. As science progresses we may break down existing laws into more basic units; in this case we may explain Boyle's law in terms of the movement of molecules of gas. Yet this still does not explain (i) *why* molecules act in this way, or (ii) why they should *always* do so. As we progress further we may talk in sub-atomic terms. Yet no matter how far we reduce to more and more basic laws, we will *never* be able to say (i) *why* things operate in this way, or (ii) why they should *always* do so. Moreover, to say 'because it is in their nature to do so' or something of this kind, in reality adds nothing more. Scientific laws may be valid or invalid, useful or useless, but ultimately are nothing more than detailed descriptions of how things normally behave. They can *never* get back to some sort of *ultimate cause* for things to behave in the ways that they do.[6]

The Christian may believe that this *ultimate cause* is God, *who holds together the universe by his word of power.*[7] It is vital to understand that this does *not* mean he provides one more force alongside other forces; it means rather that he is the ultimate *why* of *all* forces. Professor Mackay gives in his booklet an analogy of a television screen. Within the picture on the screen we may observe causes, effects, and so on, operating in certain patterns. The cause of the picture being on the screen at all is, however, not of the same order as 'causes' within the picture. God is, to the Christian, the cause of the universe continuing as it does and not merely *a* cause which operates *within* it. The Christian believes that matter operates according to scientific laws because God maintains the universe in this way. Thus when God operates in a way which differs from his normal pattern of material cause-effect, it is misleading to talk (as some do) as though he were 'interfering with' or 'intervening in' natural processes. The latter have no existence outside his moment-by-moment working in such patterns.

If the cause-effect connections were not generally predictable then life would be impossible and we could not even communicate with one another. Therefore God maintains the universe so that in general the effects of physical actions are predictable. But this need not stop him from, on occasion, varying the pattern of his working. In section (14) we outline C.S.Lewis's analogy of a game of chess. One player may sometimes be allowed to retrieve an ill-considered move, but if one player made pieces appear and disappear at will, then there could be no game at all. If God's workings were capricious and unpredictable, then the game of life would be altogether impossible. God usually works, therefore, according to a set pattern, even if occasionally it may be altered. Even when it is, Christians are not, of course, saying that there are un-caused events. The cause is God, and there is always purpose behind his action. Moreover, if Jesus were really God's unique incarnation in history as he claimed to be, then it would surely be *un*natural if there were nothing miraculous about him.

The Christian view of scientific laws, then, is that we are discovering the usual patterns which God maintains in the working of his universe, and seeking to describe these ever more accurately. In the words of a founder of modern astronomy, we are 'thinking God's thoughts after Him'. The discovery that miracles have occurred neither causes us to doubt the validity of these laws, nor gives rise to any philosophical problems.

Further Reading:

Miracles C.S.Lewis (Fontana)
'... Mr. Lewis has produced an impressive book. He has shown that it is irrational to overlook the possibility of the miraculous.' *The Times Literary Supplement.*

Christian Belief and Science R.E.D.Clark (C.U.P.)
Dr Clark is a Cambridge scientist who firmly believes that man arrives at conclusions in science and in faith by similar thought processes.

Questions of Science and Faith J.N.Hawthorne (Tyndale)
A Bio-Chemist discusses generally the relationship between science and the Christian faith.

Notes for Section 6

1. Mark 4.39.
2. John 21.4-6.
3. 1 Kings 17.4-6.
4. Exodus 7 - 10.
5. Various philosophers have analysed this question; see especially David Hume.
6. So far this is simply an outline critique of the 'essentialist' view of science, now largely abandoned by thinkers in this field. For further thought, see a standard work on the philosophy of science, e.g. Karl Popper's *Conjectures and Refutations* chapter three.
7. Hebrews 1.3 also Colossians 2.17.

SINCE WE DO NOT SEE MIRACLES TODAY, COULDN'T IT BE THAT PEOPLE USED TO BE MORE SIMPLE?

7 It is often said nowadays that people two thousand years ago were simple and credulous, whereas modern man has 'come of age'. Nevertheless, people of the Bible times seem to have been just as surprised as we should be today to see five loaves feed five thousand people, or a man walking on the water. When the angel told Mary that she was going to have a baby, her first reaction was: 'But isn't that impossible, for I have never had intercourse with anyone?'[1] The angel did not answer that it was common for virgins to give birth to sons. He replied that this baby was to be unique in history. Moreover, when Joseph discovered that his fiancée was pregnant he reacted in the same way as any modern man might.[2] He knew how pregnancies begin, and only a special vision convinced him that this one was unique. First century people like Joseph and Mary seem no more simple or ignorant of these matters than are people of today (though perhaps they were a little less arrogant about 'coming of age'). Jesus' contemporaries knew as well as we do that virgins do not conceive sons, that men do not walk on water, that five loaves will not feed five thousand, and that men born blind do not instantaneously recover their sight. Thus in recording what they themselves experience and saw, they continually showed surprise: 'Never since the world began has it been heard that anyone opened the eyes of a man born blind,' said the man to whom it had just happened![3] Some refused point-blank to accept the accounts of others about the unbelievable events. "Unless I see in his hands the print of the nails, and place my finger in the mark of the nails, and place my hand in his side, I will not believe," said Thomas.[4] When confronted by first-hand evidence Thomas's scepticism vanished. Surely those today who are sceptical of such events would find it equally difficult to maintain their scepticism in the face of first-hand evidence?

Many modern instances have been confirmed of miracles taking place in situations where there has been a dynamic faith in Christ. But even where a person today finds it difficult to deny that a miracle has occurred, *to believe the miracle is not to believe in God*. Christ never used miracles to browbeat or brainwash others into accepting God. He performed them out of compassion and because he wanted to heal and help people. They were signs of his mission to those who were willing to believe in him. They were never intended as proofs to force mental acceptance on those unwilling to set up a relationship of faith and obedience with him.

Further Reading:

I Believe in Miracles K.Kuhlman (Lakeland)
A Baptist minister recounts 21 cases of miracles in her own healing ministry.

Christ Still Healing E.Salmon (Arthur James)
Mrs Salmon's book records many incidents of healing. The characters mentioned in the remarkable case recorded in the Epilogue are known personally to one of the authors.

Revival in Indonesia K.E.Koch (Evangelisation Publishers)
A recent book which includes accounts of miracles.

Notes for Section 7

1. Luke 1.34.
2. Matthew 1.19-20.
3. John 9.32.
4. John 20.25.

MIRACLES ASIDE – DOESN'T THE BIBLE CONTAIN UNSCIENTIFIC EXPLANATIONS OF NATURAL PROCESSES?

8 As examples of Biblical accuracy Christians often point to things like Job's reference to the earth hanging upon nothing[1] or to the Bible's accurate description of the rain cycle.[2] Such examples may indeed be striking, but we should beware of reading too much into the text. After all, the Bible was not intended to be a textbook of science; what it claims to be is a revelation from God about himself and man, to all generations and types of men, whether science-conscious or not. If this claim be true, then we should not expect the Bible to contain 'scientific' explanations. On the other hand, we will not be surprised to discover that it contains none of the kinds of gross scientific errors found in other writings of its period. In early Asian and Middle Eastern literature such as that of Babylon, as well as in Plato and the other enlightened Greek Philosophers[3] one finds, alongside their flashes of insight, fanciful and sometimes ridiculous explanations of things like creation,

light and astronomy. The Bible was written over a period
of perhaps 2,000 years by some thirty different authors,
and yet it is free from idle scientific speculation of any kind.[4]
By and large it contents itself entirely with describing
natural things as they appear. Any concern in the Bible with
physical things is mainly in relation to their effect on
people. It is not concerned to describe the interaction of
physical things, or natural causation, other than to ascribe
ultimate causation to God. It was Newton, not the Bible,
who suggested that since comets moved in ellipses there
must be angels pushing them!

Notes for Section 8

1. Job 26.7.
2. Job 36.27-30; 37.11; Ecclesiastes 1.7.
3. With the possible exception of Aristarchus of Samos..
4. The archaeologist and orientalist Dr W.F.Albright wrote: 'The
   Bible towers in content above all earlier religious literature; and
   it towers just as impressively over all subsequent literature in the
   direct simplicity of its message and the catholicity of its appeal
   to men of all lands and times.' (*The Christian Century*,
   November 1958).

DOESN'T THE BIBLE ASCRIBE PSYCHOLOGICAL ILLNESS TO DEMONS?

In the first place, some Christians explain the Bible
reference to demons as a figure of speech, pointing out that
even the great psychologist Jung talked in 1945 of 'reviving
the doctrine of demons'.[1]

Secondly, most people who study the evidence become
convinced that there exists a realm of the psychic, of extra-
sensory perception, of telepathy, telekinesis, psychometry,
etc. This realm is not 'demonic' in the usual sense of the
word. It is composed simply of *natural* powers of the human
mind which are not yet understood. It is important from
the Christian point of view to grasp the distinction between
such natural powers of the mind and practices which the

Bible categorically forbids. These latter include the activities of mediums, wizards[2], and enchanters[3], divination and consulting the dead[4]. Psychic phenomena themselves only fall into this class insofar as they are associated with these forbidden activities. We must accept that such natural extra-sensory forces by themselves might account for some of the unusual manifestations both in Jesus' time and in our own.

It is our personal view, however, that neither the language of the Biblical accounts, nor indeed certain contemporary experiences, can be wholly explained using this approach. Matthew uses a different Greek word for 'possession by a demon' from that used for 'insanity'.[5] We may find absurd both the comical devil of mediaeval plays and the crude animism of some primitive societies, but this is no reason for treating as absurd the essential concept of a world of spirits. To say that science has not demonstrated such a world is naive, for the scientist is concerned with recurring physical causation, and if spirits exist that are personal and non-physical then they must by definition be excluded from the whole range of scientific study. Occasionally we meet someone who feels that we must be unbalanced or prejudiced to even suggest that there is a spirit world. But let us remember that fifty years ago it would have seemed ludicrous to suggest that invisible waves all around us could produce on a screen in our own homes a picture of a man on the moon. At the turn of the century a crude materialistic view dominated a science confident in its 'certain knowledge' and rapidly approaching omniscience. A change has occurred, perhaps stimulated by such things as the mysterious features of the Einsteinian system and the strange world of particle physics. The atmosphere in the science of today is more conducive to the admission that there may well be 'more things in heaven and earth, Horatio, than are dreamt of in our philosophy.'! It is unfortunate that the more modern open mindedness to such questions has led not merely to acknowledgement of the possible existence of spirits, but to a great resurgence in dabbling in spiritism and things of the occult. The dangers which are inherent in this have been demonstrated in such studies as that of Dr Koch, mentioned below.

Further Reading:

Christian Counselling and Occultism K.E.Koch (Kregel)
A balanced and documented demonstration of both the reality and dangers of the phenomena.

The Challenging Counterfeit R.Gasson
An assessment of the movement by an ex-spiritualist minister.

What is Man? J.Stafford Wright (Paternoster)
Psychic phenomena are included in a general investigation of what constitutes a human nature.

Psychology, Religion and Healing and *Wounded Spirits*
L.D.Weatherhead (Hodder)
Anyone interested in the subject would find these books worth reading. However, we must give here a serious warning. Although Dr Weatherhead well distinguished between the purely psychic and the demonic, he failed to emphasize certain vital points:

(a) Jesus himself obviously accepted the general authority of the Jewish Law[6] which clearly and emphatically forbids any form of mediumship or communication with the dead (see above and notes 2 - 4). Moreover, he affirmed that anyone who loved him would keep his commandments.[7] It seems clear therefore, that anyone who is truly pious in the sense of being close to Jesus Christ, would have no more wish to be a medium than to be a gangster. Apparent piety of mediums, or even genuine sincerity, should not mislead us. Whether such activities be explained scientifically, spiritistically, or in any other way, they are clearly not pursuits approved by the Christian God.

(b) To the Christian who takes God's warnings seriously, involvement in the activities mentioned in (a) is out of the question. One who makes no claim to be a Christian may wonder why he should pay any attention to 'God's warning'. However, as Koch and others have shown, dabblers in spiritism risk becoming trapped in powers beyond their control, powers which may dehumanize them or lead to mental disorder. Many who began out of a mild curiosity have found themselves drawn into something from which they cannot escape Anyone who contemplates seeking some spiritist experience should keep his eyes open to the risks involved. (See also sections 25 and 26.)

(c) The use of *natural* extra-sensory gifts (e.g. telepathy) which are *not* connected with spiritism, is not actually forbidden in the Bible. However, experience shows that:
  (i) their development may lead to mental disturbance in some people;
  (ii) in practice, they are often today associated with activities which *are* forbidden to Christians; so that development of them may all too easily lead into such things.

Notes for Section 9

1. Interview in *Weltwoche*, May 11th 1945.
2. Leviticus 19.31; 20.6,27; Deuteronomy 18.11; 2 Kings 21.6; 1 Chronicles 10.13; 2 Chronicles 33.6; Isaiah 19.3.
3. Deuteronomy 18.10; 2 Kings 21.6; 2 Chronicles 33.6; Isaiah 19.3.
4. Deuteronomy 18.10-11.
5. Matthew 4.24.
6. Matthew 5.19; 15.3; 19.17; Mark 10.19; Luke 18.20—see also section 12.
7. John 14.15.

DOES THIS MEAN THAT YOU TAKE THE BIBLE LITERALLY - ADAM AND EVE AND ALL ?

10 One must always remember our common use of pictures. We 'see a point', or 'grasp an opportunity'. We 'feel shattered', or 'become brokenhearted'—conditions not obvious from a post mortem! The scientist describing subatomic physics, as well as the poet talking of his love, may use images from the physical world of our senses, and no one asks either of them if he 'means it literally'. Likewise the Bible refers to the 'arm of God'; yet the writer could not have 'meant it literally' since in the very first section of the Bible[1] the reason given for prohibiting images is that God's form is unknown. Similarly a God 'up there' and 'above the bright blue sky' might be taken literally by a three-year-old[2] but thinking Christians down the ages have understood that God must speak to us of 'higher things' in a figurative way.

Thus it is impossible to give a simple 'Yes' or 'No' answer to the question 'Do you take the Bible literally?' We take it literally when it intends us to do so, and not otherwise. Sometimes it may be difficult to determine which way the writer did intend it to be taken. But when it says: 'mountains skipped like rams,'[3] or 'the floods clap their hands,'[4] it is presumably figurative; whereas such accounts as that of the empty tomb and the grave clothes without a body were obviously meant to be taken literally.

The question of how much is figurative in the Genesis story of creation is a more difficult one. The Hebrew word of 'day' (*yom*) seems to be used loosely; in Genesis chapter one, for example, creation is performed in six days whereas in chapter two it speaks of '*the day* in which the Lord created heaven and earth.' At least as early as Origen (A.D. 184-254) Christians have taught quite reasonably that the days are not literal days of 24 hours, so why should we disagree? To God a thousand years are as one day[5] and time has a different significance for him from what it has to us.

Since the nineteenth century, one of the most popular red herrings sidetracking those considering whether the Christian faith is true, has been its supposed conflict with the theory of evolution. For one thing the evidence for evolution is less than most schoolbooks seem to suggest; professional biologists who have shown this include, for example Professor Kerkut,[6] who is certainly no lover of church dogmatics. As well as statistical problems and fossil gaps, there is the more general problem that no observation could even be conceived, which would finally either demonstrate or refute such a theory. This fact was noted by Sir Arthur Keith, who wrote the preface to the 1928 edition of Darwin's *The Origin of Species*: 'Evolution is unproved and unprovable. We believe it because the only alternative is special creation which is unthinkable.' In the preface to the

1956 and 1963 centenary edition of *The Origin of Species* Professor Thompson wrote of 'the elusive character of the Darwinian argument; . . its very nature gives it a kind of immunity to disproof.' He explains that, although any conceivable observation whatsoever may be made to fit it, its plausibility should not be mistaken for proof; and its immunity to disproof does not mean that it must therefore be true.

But the scientific question as to whether and how evolution occurred, interesting as it is, is in any case of little importance to the Christian faith. The fossil record matches Genesis chapter one closely enough, whatever the means by which successive stages of organic life appeared. The Bible language was intended to explain the origin and significance of events. As such it gives a beautiful and valid description of creation, without discussing the actual mechanism of its development. Evolution as a scientific theory can never become a philosophy of life as some have tried to make it, nor can it ever determine whether events occurred by design or by 'chance'. Thus, many biologists have concluded that some form of scientific theory of evolution is compatible with the Bible account of creation.

In considering such questions we should recognize the background of Hebrew custom and thought. For example, the order of events was considered of less importance than the fact that they occurred and the significance of them. The early church never imagined that the Gospels record events in strict chronological order. The scholar Eusebius in book 39 of his *History of the Church* (c A.D.325) quoted from very early sources to explain that Mark took down notes from Peter's teaching about what Jesus said, *'not in order'* but *'taking care to leave out nothing that he heard and to make no mis-statement about it.'* In taking such considerations as this into account (see also section 18) we are in no way detracting from Bible accuracy, but simply trying to understand it in the way the writers intended. As we try to do this, we may find interesting a suggestion concerning the use of word patterns in Genesis chapter one which is hinted at in Dr Kidner's commentary and analysed by Dr Filby. This views the second three days of the creation story as an explanation and expansion of the first three, indicating that the writer may not have intended to convey six literally successive time periods.

On the question itself of Adam and Eve, the Bible has been interpreted in various ways by Christians. Some have asserted that Adam and Eve were literally the first humans. Others have suggested that men existed before Adam, but that to him God first gave a spirit. We find attractive the suggestion of E.K.V.Pearce that the hunter-gatherers of Genesis chapter one were succeeded by the agriculturalists of the Neolithic revolution, described in chapter two. However, any firm decision on this type of issue is made difficult by the differences which exist between the supposed lines of descent for man which are supplied by different experts in the field. Moreover, the often used criterion of brain capacity may be misleading, since intelligence is not necessarily proportional to this.[8] Such considerations make us hestitate before coming to any definite conclusions about Adam, given the present state of knowledge. We may, however, accept that all modern men descend from a single origin; a Cambridge Professor of Archaeology wrote in 1961: 'The overwhelming consensus of professional opinion is that the existing races of mankind are without exception variants of this single species *Homo Sapiens*.'[9] The scientist may use Latin and call this original source *Homo Sapiens*, but the Hebrew name for him, *Adam*,[10] is surely just as valid.

In any event, the first chapter or so of Genesis is a remarkable account, unique in ancient writings, and it is fitting that it should have been read by the astronauts as they conducted man's first flight around the moon.

Further Reading:

Who Was Adam? E.K.Victor Pearce (Paternoster)
The Origin of Man E.K.Victor Pearce (Crusade Reprint)
E.K.V.Pearce read anthropology and human origins at University and he here investigates the relationship between his studies and the early chapters of Genesis.

Creation Revealed F. Filby (Pickering and Inglis)
Dr Filby offers some useful suggestions for the understanding of Genesis chapter one.

Questions of Science and Faith J.N.Hawthorne (Tyndale)
This includes a brief discussion of evolution in its relation to the Christian faith.

Genesis, An Introduction and Commentary Derek Kidner (Tyndale)
In the context of a general commentary on Genesis many of the possible interpretations of the creation account are briefly considered.

Genesis One Reconsidered D.Payne (Tyndale)
The writer shows how we should approach Genesis theologically and not scientifically; he also compares it with other early accounts of origins.

Notes for Section 10

1. Deuteronomy 4.15-19, which is in the Pentateuch i.e. the first five books.

2. And apparently also by some inhabitants of a certain Southbank Diocese in the 1960's!

3. Psalm 114.4.

4. Psalm 98.8.

5. Psalm 90.4; 2 Peter 3.8.

6. *Implications of Evolution* (Pergamon)

7. Experts in this field (which is the field of one of the authors of this book) are today debating what the meaning of the word *chance* really is.

8. Incidentally, Cro-Magnon man was built like a Greek god, and had an average brain capacity of 1750 ccs; the average for a modern European is a mere 1500 ccs!

9. Dr G.Clark: *World Prehistory, An Outline* p.23.

10. *Adam* is a general Hebrew word meaning either 'man' or 'red' and coming from the same general root as 'earth'. There is no distinct plural form and so the word *Adam* may be individual or corporate. This double meaning is utilised by Paul in his comments on *the New Man* in Romans chapters 5 and 6. A detailed discussion of the degree of symbolism implicit in Genesis chapter 1 would be rewarding, but is beyond the scope of this book.

EVEN IF THE BIBLE IS NOT WRONG ON SPECIFIC POINTS, IS NOT THE WHOLE VIEW OF THE WORLD ACCORDING TO SCIENCE A DIFFERENT ONE?

11

As human beings we are conscious of two realms: the physical realm incorporating length, weight, movement, etc, and the 'personal' realm incorporating love, hate, morality, personality, etc.[1] It is philosophically possible to deny the existence of either of these. The solipsist denies the reality of the first and says that all is an illusion; the logical positivist believes that words like 'love' and 'personality' are meaningless[2] and, in effect, denies the reality of the second. Now the place of science is only to describe what normally happens in the *physical* world; therefore, to say (as some have done) that the scientific description is the *only valid one* is simply to deny the existence or the reality of the personal realm. It is possible to do this, but in practice very few do so consistently. Our self-consciousness and our experience of emotion tend to compel in us a belief in more than the purely physical realm, no matter what theories we may try to erect.

These comments apply in particular to those psychologists (and it is certainly not all of that profession) who take a deterministic view of man, seeing him as nothing more than a highly complex machine. Such a view is by no means proven, and since at present we know so little about the strange extra-sensory powers of some minds, it would, on scientific grounds, be rash to hold it dogmatically. But a more serious criticism of those who believe it is that one often finds them slipping into moral statements such as: 'It is wrong to condemn people for acts of crime, since they cannot help themselves.' There is a logical inconsistency here. Suppose that I do condemn a criminal, how can it be 'wrong' if (as they imply) my own action was merely a deterministic result of the state of my brain, and so can involve no moral choice? Even in attacking traditional moral structures (which may admittedly leave much to be desired) they still find themselves using moral concepts; the idea of morality seems to be deeply ingrained in human experience. Theoretically one could believe in a system of pure materialism (positivist, dialectic, or otherwise) and deny any reality to moral concepts and personality. Such a view would have no logical flaws within it, but very few people, if any, seem to have believed it consistently. Man seems unable to escape from moral concepts. Moreover, the various attempts to give meaning to these solely on a basis of (a) *nature* or (b) *reason* or (c) *social convenience* are each of them unconvincing, for the following reasons:[3]

(a) For a Theist the word *natural* may imply the functioning of something in the way that its designer intended. For the materialist, all that exists is nature, and so anything that happens must be 'natural'. Thus if 'nature' is the basis of morality, then everything that man does is right.

(b) *Reason* is that in us which enables us to understand relations between different scientific and/or historical propositions. Also, given some fundamental moral axiom, reason may be used to elucidate how this axiom applies in any concrete circumstance. What reason can never do is provide the ultimate basis for our moral axioms. It is a tool, but never a source of morality. (Incidentally, even if used in this, its proper role, reason cannot be relied upon by a materialist. If his brain is purely a chemical result of chance mutations and development, then it must have a survival value for him, but need not necessarily be reliable in matters of truth.)

(c) The only remaining basis for materialist morality would be *social convenience*, perhaps as classically expressed in the various 'social contract' theories. However, these could never give the individual any reason to continue behaving socially should it become more profitable to him personally to do otherwise.[4] Nor would society need to consider the 'rights' of minorities or individuals. Morality, in such a case, becomes only another name for selfishness worked out collectively. Certainly this cannot logically explain the readiness of many of its materialist adherents to suffer, and even die, in their cause.

If, then, we were to accept that the scientific description of the world was the *only* valid one, we would be faced with a problem in defining morality. There would also be a problem surrounding the origin of personality itself. If a man is merely a product of time plus chance plus impersonal forces, how then can he have personhood? A behaviourist may tell us that 'personality' is a word merely describing how a particular human being in fact reacts—but is this really very satisfactory? The physiologist can explain the neurochemical action of bananas on the taste buds of the tongue, but this does not 'explain' the subjective experience of that taste to us. Unlike electronic computers we are *aware* that we are each a centre of consciousness—we *experience* that we have personhood as something over and above mere reactions to stimuli. If there is indeed a personal Creator who made man in his image, then we can see how this personhood could be valid. But if one rejects a personal God, and yet wants somehow to keep morality and a meaning for life on a purely materialistic basis, how can this possibly be done? One is left with recourse to irrational mysticism or some other totally blind leap of faith.

If we accept a Christian view of the world then these problems are much reduced. Christianity *is* concerned with the physical, for Christ healed bodies as well as minds; but this concern is mainly at the point where physical things are affecting *people*. The prior concern of the Christian faith is with the world of persons and moral relationships which stems from the personal God. The scientific study of the purely physical is thus not excluded or contradicted in any way, for it may form a valuable part of a Christian outlook. Historically, many scientists have found that their belief in a rational and loving Creator was, if anything, a positive help in their work. Moreover, the popular belief that history is littered with scientists persecuted and harassed by the Church is erroneous. One documented study of the subject says: 'Giordano Bruno and Michael Servatus (burned in 1553 by the Calvinists in Geneva) seem to be the only scholars of repute who became victims of religious intolerance in the sixteenth and seventeenth centuries—not, of course, because of their scientific, but because of their religious opinions.'[5] The same study describes as 'naively erroneous' the idea that the trial of Galileo was 'a showdown between "blind faith" and "enlightened reason".'[6] On the contrary the relations were extremely good and the vast majority of great early scientists (e.g. Kepler, Boyle and Newton) placed great emphasis on their faith. Dr Clark of Cambridge goes as far as to write: 'There is little doubt that the scientific movement of the seventeenth century owed its origin to the Christian faith.'[7] In a short chronicle of the vast number of great scientists who had sincere faith, Professor Dixon writes: 'It is very interesting to note how greatly the development of physics in the 19th and early 20th centuries was due to this group of deeply religious men, Kelvin, Rayleigh, Maxwell, Stokes and Thompson.'[8]

The scientific view of the world should form an integral part of the whole Christian viewpoint, for it in no way conflicts with it. When science has, in the past, been found in this role, it has proved singularly productive.

Further Reading:

There is useful literature on this subject from a number of angles:

(i) Views of Practising Scientists:

Faith and the Physical World D.L.Dye (Paternoster)
Dr Dye, physicist, outlines his comprehensive world view incorporating the presuppositions of both science and faith.

Science and Irreligion Malcolm Dixon (Falcon)
Dr Dixon is an ScD, F.R.S. and co-author of a standard university text. His booklet is one of the clearest short outlines of how faith and science are related.

Science and Christian Faith Today D.M.Mackay (Falcon)
Professor Mackay of Keele University outlines his views on the relationship of God to the material world.

(ii) The Philosophical Approach:

The Abolition of Man C.S.Lewis (Bles)
Professor C.S.Lewis considers the problems of preserving meaning to morality and values outside the Christian belief system.

The God Who is There Francis Schaeffer (Hodder)
Dr Schaeffer sketches some of the problems of values in modern art and philosophy, caused by abandonment of belief in an objective God.

(iii) The Psychological and Parapsychological Approach:

The Meaning of Persons Paul Tournier (S.C.M.)
Dr Tournier, a Geneva psychiatrist, explains how his understanding of life's meaning is tied up with the meaning of persons.

What Is Man? J.Stafford Wright (Paternoster)
The author presents some of the evidences about various constituents of the nature of man.

Notes for Section 11

1. This is not necessarily to deny any correlation between physical brain states and emotions.

2. Or at best phenomenalogical.

3. See also C.S.Lewis *The Abolition of Man*.

4. Not all of us are motivated by Hobbe's obsessive fear of death!

5. *The Sleepwalkers* by Arthur Koestler, p.451.

6. p.432; This whole book is worth reading, see for example p.358:
   'Contrary to statements in even recent outlines of science, Galileo. . . made no contribution to theoretical astronomy; he did not throw down weights from the leaning tower of Pisa, and did not prove the Copernican system. He was not tortured by the inquisition, did not lament in its dungeons, did not say "*eppur si muove*"; and he was not a martyr of science. What he *did* was to found the modern science of dynamics'.
   In a similar vein the philosopher and mathematician Professor A.N.Whitehead F.R.S. wrote: 'In the generation which saw the Thirty Years War and remembered Alva in the Netherlands, the worst that happened to men of science was that Galileo suffered an honorable detention and a mild reproof before dying peaceably in his bed.'

7. *Christian Belief and Science* p.64.

8. *Science and Irreligion* p.7.

CHRISTIANS OFTEN SEEM TO ME TO ARGUE IN CIRCLES!

12 Christians do unfortunately sometimes give this impression, and one hears questioners assert it over various issues. One issue of this kind stimulates the accusation: *You solve the origin of the world by calling it God, but now tell me where God came from?* This is different from most of the 'circular' problems in that it is purely intellectual, and it is therefore dealt with in the next section. The other problems nearly all concern in some way or another the relationship of *faith* and *reason*; we must therefore first discuss this general issue before proceeding to some specific questions which involve circular arguments.

In some religious circles *faith* seems to be viewed as believing the irrational, and *reason* is regarded as something almost unchristian! Such a view would have seemed strange indeed to the apostles. Their continual practice was to *argue* and *dispute* in the synagogues and debating centres (Acts 6.9-10; 9.29; 17.2,17; 18.4,19; 19.8,9; 24.25). In this they would begin from wherever their listeners stood, and argue from that basis. Thus, in Jewish synagogues they would quote the Scriptures as an authority.[1] When Paul spoke to the University at Athens he quoted the classical writers.[2] To the common non-Hebrew crowd Paul talked of everyday things and led from this to the Creator.[3] Thus the apostles began from wherever their listeners stood; and we may be sure that their arguments were rational enough to confute many expert opponents.[4] Moreover, the office of apostleship involved witnessing to Jesus' resurrection,[5] to what they had actually seen and heard of him.[6] Faith was quite rightly based on firm objective evidence—Jesus was risen!

In our own day and age Christians should be able to give to questioners the objective evidence concerning Christ and Christianity.[7] It is in this belief that we have given a sketch of such evidence in the preceding parts of this book. The arguments are historical and scientific, and nowhere demand any sort of blind faith. In discussion we would try, as did the apostles, to begin from wherever a person stands—taking into account, for example, his attitude to the Bible.

We believe then, that those Christians who are so extremely suspicious about reason and rational arguments are not following the apostolic example. There is, however, an element of justification for their suspicions, for rational argument and intellectual belief alone cannot of themselves make a person into a Christian. Becoming a Christian involves a conscious act whereby one communicates to God a desire to do his will (see sections 27 and 29). Reason can help us to see how such an act of committal is meaningful, but it cannot make the act for us; this is a matter of the conscience[8] and the will.

After a person has taken such a step as this, he finds that his subjective experiences of God confirm to his heart the truth of Christianity. Both the objective evidence and his subjective experience now point to the existence of God. Moreover, as his relationship with God develops, God helps him to understand more of his truth. Thus understanding and knowledge of God increase. But there is never anything *irrational* about such understanding or knowledge. Perhaps what has led to misunderstanding on this score is the fact that the basic business of being a Christian is seeking God's will and loving him and others—all of which activities are practical rather than intellectual. They are not *anti-*intellectual activities, but they are activities which the unintellectual as well as the intellectual can follow. Few of us would wish this otherwise, for if it were, then the intellectual would have a very unfair advantage. In actual fact, to love others involves a renouncement of pride and of materialism which is often found very difficult by someone from a privileged group—whether clever or rich; the Bible observes, therefore, how difficult it is for a rich man to be saved[9] and it is more often the poor and foolish who become the chosen.[10] It is less arduous to pursue God in intellect than it is to pursue him in experience, for the latter requires humility, love, selflessness and obedience for its full attainment. And yet it is surely foolishness to acquire much wisdom and knowledge of truth if we baulk at committal to Christ who *is* the truth.[11]

Faith then, is a relationship, and not mere acceptance of

a set of axioms. Nevertheless faith is quite rational and reasonable. With this in mind we may look at several problems which are sometimes raised:

(i) You tell me to believe in the authority of the Bible; yet I cannot accept that authority unless I already believe.

(ii) You can only point to texts in the Bible itself to prove that it is inspired.

There is no need for Christians to argue with non-Christians over the Bible's authority. If we meet a non-Christian who rejects that authority, then we find it best to try to understand where he stands, and begin discussion from this point without becoming entangled in arguments about the Bible's inspiration. This usually means that we can agree that historical documents known as the Gospels exist, and that they claim to record the life of a man called Jesus. A person who rejects any idea of Biblical authority must nevertheless face the sort of questions which were raised in sections 2 to 5 of this book, about the documents and the one they claim to describe. To such a person we might quote a Bible verse in order to illustrate what Jesus Christ taught on some subject, but there would, of course, be little point in quoting it to 'prove' the truth of what it asserts. In other words, the whole set of documents which we call the Bible would provide part of the data for discussion, but not a source of unsupported dogma. Moreover, as Christians we believe that the person with whom we discuss is God's creature, and God may speak to his heart if he reads the Bible sincerely, whether or not he believes it to be inspired. Thus, in making a point in discussion, we might use the words of God recorded in the Bible because we believe that there is a certain power in them. Christians must, however, beware of the danger of churlishly repeating texts, unrelated to their hearer's need or position, in the vain hope that the words will somehow work like a magic charm!

We ourselves do accept the authority and inspiration of the Bible, but this is certainly not simply because it claims such a thing for itself! Such a claim, and the prophets' claim to speak with God's voice, are outrageous enough to make us want to consider them and decide their validity—but they certainly do not prove the case. Our reasons for accepting the Bible are in fact partly objective and partly subjective. On the objective side, Jesus himself accepted the Old Testament as inspired[12]. If we are at all to accept his often repeated claim that he always spoke God's message, then it seems only logical to accept what he implies about the scriptures. Thus a belief in the Old Testament logically comes together with acceptance of the claims of Jesus about himself. (For points about the accuracy of the records of Jesus see section 4.) As to the New Testament, Jesus also promised his disciples that the Holy Spirit would help them to remember his teachings, and would guide them into further truth.[13] Thus we believe that the books written under their authority may be accepted as reliable. Historically we discover that such books may be fairly easily identified as those of the New Testament.[14] This explains then why belief in the Bible's authority logically comes together with acceptance of Christ's claims.[15] The argument would only become circular if one had to believe in the Bible's authority in order to believe in Christ or become a Christian, and this is not so. (See also section 28.)

On a more subjective and experiential level, anyone who loves God and wants to follow him should surely ask God himself what he thinks about the Bible. In the experience of the present authors God reaffirms to Christians the authority which he gives the Bible (though see section 18 for some comment on how it is meant to be approached). This is not an objective 'proof' which we could present to others, but illustrates the points made earlier about the subjective and the objective going along together. Our experience confirms what our reason tells us and our reason confirms our experience. There is nothing contradictory about it, and nothing circular in the argument.

(iii) You say that if I become a Christian then I will be certain that God exists; but surely I must believe that he exists in order to become a Christian?

(iv) You say that I will be able to understand better if I am a Christian; but unless I understand, how can I become one?

Becoming a Christian involves our making an act of committal to Christ, and asking God (if he exists) to come into our lives. For anyone to do this he must at least admit the possibility that God might exist, and must have some understanding of what the Christian Gospel says, but he need not be certain that God is there nor need he understand completely.[16] What is important is that he acts on the basis of what he does know and what he does understand (see section 29). We have known atheists who have prayed something like this: 'God, if there is a God, I want to believe on you and do your will.' Then, as they began seriously to read through the New Testament, they discovered that their prayer had been answered. No doubt it may make it easier to take a step of committal if one believes God is there, and understands well what is involved. Nevertheless, God is really interested in a sincere desire to follow him, not in correct beliefs or understanding.

When someone takes the step of becoming a Christian, his day-by-day experience of God is certain to lead to an increased assurance and understanding of him. There is nothing in this which is contrary to reason. It does not, moreover, affect the possibility of committal being made before such assurance and understanding comes. There is no true circular thinking in Christianity's appeal for a step of faith.

Further Reading:

Our Lord's View of the Old Testament John W.Wenham (I.V.F.)
A very useful and concise short outline of this important topic, considering it in the context of its implications.

Notes for Section 12

1. e.g. Acts 17.2-3.
2. Acts 17.28: he quotes Aratus the Stoic (*Phaenom*.1-5; Stobaeus: *Eclogae Physicae* 1.7) though the words resemble Cleanthe's *Hymn to Zeus*; he also quotes from Epimenides the Cretan (see notes 11 and 12 to section 20).
3. Acts 14.15.
4. Acts 9.22.
5. Acts 1.22; 1 Corinthians 15.7-9.
6. 1 John 1.1.
7. 1 Peter 3.15, and remember that Peter himself was by no means an intellectual!

8. The word *conscience* is, incidentally, not an anti-scientific concept. In his famous book *Man, Morals and Society* the psychologist J.C.Flugel writes: 'the existence of something corresponding to the popular idea of 'conscience' had been demonstrated by the most precise methods at present available.' (p.30; 1962 edition.)

9. Matthew 19.24; Mark 10.25; Luke 18.25.

10. 1 Corinthians 1.27-29.

11. Paul puts this pungently in 1 Corinthians 1.21.

12. Matthew 5.17-19; see also Wenham's book.

13. John 14.26; this is the most clear explicit promise, but the statement need not be based on this text alone. There is, in the Gospels, a larger theme of Jesus' choice of the apostles and conferment of authority upon them.

14. Mainly due to difficulties of communication and the scattered nature of the early church, various reservations were held about different parts of the New Testament in different places and at different times. Some reservations were held about 2 and 3 John and Jude, but the only real doubt anywhere seems to have been over 2 Peter and Revelation, and the only non-New Testament books accorded any measure of authority were the epistles of Clement and Barnabas and the Shepherd of Hermas. We may also note the veneration in which leading Christians of the late first century and second century held the apostles, and the distinctions they made between apostolic writings and their own: see 1 Clement (c.95-96) 3.12-16; 19.1-3; 20.22; Ignatius to Rome (c.110) 2.6; Polycarp to Philippi (c.150) 2.2.

15. Dr W.F.Albright writes: 'To the writers of the New Testament the Hebrew Bible was Holy Scripture and they were the direct heirs of its prophets. It is, accordingly, quite impossible to understand the New Testament without recognizing that its purpose was to supplement and explain the Hebrew Bible. Any attempt to go back to the sources of Christianity without accepting the entire Bible as our guide is thus doomed to failure.'

16. The words in Hebrews 11.6 are not, of course, addressed to anyone becoming a Christian. They are addressed to Christians, with the purpose of emphasizing that the sort of life which is pleasing to God is the one which is lived in a day by day reliance on him. In this context a person obviously has to believe in God's power and rely on it.

WHERE DID GOD COME FROM, AND WHAT DID HE DO BEFORE THE UNIVERSE BEGAN?

13 No one who is familiar with scientific thought since Einstein, needs to ask this kind of question. If things start to travel at very high speeds then time, we discover, can be 'bent', slowed down or speeded up. Though our minds cannot really grasp this, it at least makes it easier to accept the apparent Biblical teaching that God is outside of time.[1] If God *is* outside of time, then to ask when he began or who made him and how he then occupied himself is seen to be meaningless. Either question assumes as a basis something which is not true, namely, that God exists within our time. It is like asking: "When did William the Conqueror discover America?"!

As to the question of origins itself, we may note that logically there are but three possibilities:

(a) Only a material Universe exists, and it has always existed.

(b) Only a material Universe exists, and it began out of nothing.

(c) A spiritual God who is outside of time created both our material universe and time itself.

On rational grounds we find (b) frankly incredible. This leaves us with only two alternatives, and both are difficult for our limited minds to imagine. View (a) however, involves a serious intellectual problem: According to the laws of thermo-dynamics, energy levels within different parts of a closed system tend to become uniform. *Given infinite time*, energy levels throughout the closed system of the universe should eventually become uniform, and all energy/matter become reduced to its simplest form.[2] Thus, unless our present scientific understanding be radically altered, it would be difficult to hold view (a) as an explanation of a universe in which energy levels are manifestly *not* uniform.

The usual criticism made of view (c) is that it merely moves the problem back by one stage. The question "Who made the world?" is answered "God did," and the foolish Christians do not realize that this merely transforms the relevant question into: "Who made God?"! If, however, we consider this more carefully, we may discover that this criticism is unfounded. Our material world is observably subject both to time and to the laws of thermo-dynamics, whereas God is subject to neither. Thus if matter is all that exists, then we must either answer the question of how it started or else face the one of why it hasn't run down yet. If, on the other hand, we posit a timeless and spiritual God, then to ask how he started is meaningless and to ask why he hasn't run down is unnecessary.

Thus we may see that the Christian belief in God as creator *does* contribute something real towards answering the problem of origins. Moreover, the Christian's inability to answer such questions as "Where did God come from?" and "What did he do before the universe began?" is seen to be a result neither of his own ignorance nor of any fault in his belief-system, but of the meaninglessness of the questions themselves.

Notes for Section 13

1. Psalm 90.4 and 2 Peter 3.8; Colossians 1.17; Proverbs 8.23 LXX 'He established me before time was in the beginning.'
2. Christians have sometimes misused the laws of thermo-dynamics in contexts where they do not logically apply. The essential points in this context, in which we think they *do* apply, are that it is both a closed system and runs for infinite time.

IS IT RATIONAL TO BELIEVE THAT A GOD OF LOVE COULD CREATE A UNIVERSE AS FULL OF PAIN AS OURS?

14 Christians believe that God is Love. He wanted to create a person (and thus a race) with whom he could enter into a reciprocated love-relationship. Without freedom of choice, however, love would be a meaningless thing. One may have a love relationship with a person who has free will, but not with a robot operating at one's own command. If, however, you and I possess free will, then the possibility of our rejecting God and going our own way must be real in every sense and not merely apparent. Thus the possibility of evil is inherent in the very existence of freedom. When for the first time a free being rejected God and Love, and chose instead selfishness and evil, he was not choosing some entity 'evil' which God had created. In the very act of choice he created his own evil. *God is light, and in him there is no darkness at all.*[1] If that first sinner constructed a little box inside which it was dark, this does not mean that he went and gathered some darkness from somewhere to box up. He only had to shut out the light to leave darkness—even supposing that none had ever existed before.

God gave the original man a choice between the tree of life—the life which is in Christ[2]—and the tree of the experimental knowledge of good and evil. Though God had warned him of the consequences, nevertheless man chose wrongly, and it became necessary for Christ to give his life to make the tree of life available for all other generations. Much of the pain since that first human choice has been the result of the wrongness of men. People often ask: "Why doesn't God stop the war in So-and-so?" But consider: if God stopped all the trouble and all the evil in the world, then he would be compelled to eradicate you and me, for in us too there is evil which is a source of suffering for others, not to mention ourselves.

Someone may now protest: "But I thought that nothing

was supposed to be impossible to God. Then why should he not have created free beings certain to resist temptation?" It is true that Christians believe in the power of God, but we must not put 'God can' in front of nonsense and pretend that it means something. To say "God can create a free being predetermined to do right" is as meaningless as to say: "God can make a tripod with four legs."

It is man's abuse of the free will which God has given him that has led to so much suffering in the world. C.S.Lewis further observes: 'We can, perhaps, conceive of a world in which God corrected the results of this abuse of free will by his creatures at every moment: so that a wooden beam became soft as grass when it was used as a weapon, and the air refused to obey me if I attempted to set up in it the sound waves that carry lies or insults. But such a world would be one in which wrong actions were impossible, and in which, therefore, freedom of the will would be void; . . . All matter in the neighbourhood of a wicked man would be liable to undergo unpredictable alterations. That God can and does, on occasions, modify the behaviour of matter and produce what we call miracles is part of the Christian faith; but the very conception of a common, and therefore stable, world, demands that these occasions should be extremely rare.'[3] Professor Lewis goes on to give the analogy of a chess game. One player may allow the other occasionally to take back a move made inadvisedly, but there must still be rules to the game. If one player could make pieces appear and disappear at will, then there could be no game at all. If we are to exist at all as real persons, then it must be in some kind of universe in which there are fixed laws and a fixed medium of communication. Although God may occasionally perform miracles, he still in general upholds what we might call scientific laws. If he did not, then persons could not exist at all. In order to create persons with free will there had to be a predictable universe, and because of man's rebellion one of the inescapable consequences of this was suffering, whether mental or physical.

Some may wonder whether, if the price for the existence of freedom and love has been suffering and pain, it might have been better not to create anything at all. In our view there does not exist any possible basis on which to judge this kind of question. How does one weigh an hour of joy or love against an hour of sorrow or pain? St Paul felt that *the sufferings of this present time are not worth comparing with the glory that is to be revealed to us*,[4] and he certainly suffered enough.[5] Whether or not we feel in agreement with him, we should at least be prepared to admit that, in our present inevitably limited perspective, this kind of imponderable question need not deter us from considering the claims of the one who himself suffered on the cross.

Further Reading:

The Problem of Pain C.S.Lewis (Fontana)
Professor Lewis's book is now a classic, and still probably the best in this field.

The Problem of Suffering E.John Smith (Walter)
A short booklet concerning the Aberfan tragedy.

Notes for Section 14

1. 1 John 1.5.
2. Genesis 2.9, 16-17; Revelation 2.7; 22.2, 14, 19.
3. *The Problem of Pain*
4. Romans 8.18.
5. 2 Corinthians 11.24-28.

WHAT ABOUT DISEASE, IS THAT A RESULT OF SIN?

15

The book of Job makes it quite clear that people do not become sick because they have been more wicked than others, and Christ also affirms this.[1] There does, however, seem good reason to believe that God intended the relationship between the body and the mind of man to be quite different from what it is. We never read of Christ being sick. Moreover he healed others; and the apostles and some Christians ever since have also been able to do so. Illnesses which are plainly psychological, and physical ailments with ultimate psychological origins, would never have occurred in a universe in harmony with God. But we further believe that the natural psychic or extra-sensory powers of a man fully in tune with the God of love would have precluded the possibility of any illness at all. How can we imagine what the situation would have been like if man had fulfilled the command to subdue the earth[2], instead of losing his vital link with God which made this possible? Perhaps in such conditions, all things, including the bacteria which cause disease, would have functioned in harmony as God intended.

Further Reading:

The Problem of Pain C.S.Lewis (Fontana)
A standard text for this subject.

What Is Man? J.Stafford Wright (Paternoster)
A full understanding of all that man's nature involves will help us to see how God intended him to function.

The Healing of Persons Paul Tournier (Collins)
A Doctor's Casebook in the Light of the Bible
Paul Tournier (S.C.M.)
The problem of this section is discussed in many of Dr Tournier's books, including these two.

Psychology, Religion and Healing L.Weatherhead (Hodder)
Dr Weatherhead's books contain some material relevant to this section; but we would stress again the provisos at the end of section 9.

Notes for Section 15

1. John 9.1-3; Luke 13.1-5.
2. Genesis 1.28.

WHAT OF THE ANIMAL WORLD, WHERE THERE IS SO MUCH KILLING AND SUFFERING?

16 Christians differ over the question of when the pain in our world began. Some believe that it began when Adam fell. Others believe that Satan had already introduced disorder into the world in general, and that Adam was placed in a localized garden paradise in the area of Eden;[1] in this case man was possibly intended to subdue the earth and rectify its affairs. The question is a difficult one, for in the present disordered state of things it is difficult to see quite how God intended all nature to inter-react. In any event it is clear that the created world is not all that it should be or was intended to be[2] and that one day there is to be a transformation symbolized by *the wolf dwelling with the lamb*.[3]

Further Reading:

The Problem of Pain C.S.Lewis (Fontana)
In chapter nine Professor Lewis considers this aspect of pain and suffering.

Notes for Section 16

1. Genesis 2.8.
2. Romans 8.21-22.
3. Isaiah 11.6-10.

WHAT WOULD YOU SAY TO ONE WHO IS ACTUALLY SUFFERING?

17

One might outline some of the points above, and explain that God's ideal plan would have been quite different—but this alone is unlikely to be sufficient. C.S.Lewis wrote *The Problem of Pain* and then, years later, he lost his own beloved wife through a painful cancer. His theoretical answers seemed cold and impersonal in the face of his own grief. His subsequent book *A Grief Observed* records his thoughts jotted down during that time. The most comforting consideration may be that God himself is not merely an observer, but actually enters into the sufferings of mankind. When Jesus saw the sorrow in Bethany over the death of Lazarus he wept. He himself knew what he would do, but it hurt him to see reflected in that situation all the sorrow and bereavement in the world[1]. The one who was prophetically portrayed as the 'Suffering Servant' was, like God his Father, afflicted in our afflictions[2]. As we know, this 'man of sorrows' who was 'acquainted with grief' ended his own life in the agony of flogging and crucifixion. God was prepared to go to such extreme lengths to offer a love relationship to man, for God is Love. The Christian who is in pain may receive great consolation from this fact that God loves him. Incidentally, we may notice that Christianity is the only religion or belief-system which gives this sort of answer to the problem of pain. To the pantheist, good and evil, pleasure and pain, are all equally part of God; thus the Hindu God is indifferent to human suffering. The Moslem God enacts his sovereign will in determining all occurrences, whether pleasant or unpleasant, and thus he is *above* all human suffering. The only answer to pain which is offered by Buddhism is the extinction of the 'personal self' which feels it. Christianity seems to be unique in that it both maintains a meaning to personality and presents a personal God who suffers with us his creatures.

In our experience, the number of people who turn

against God because of their own suffering is less than many who have not suffered tend to imagine. On the contrary, we know of many who in suffering found that God was concerned and suffered with them. Thus they found through their experiences a deeper faith in him. We do not believe that God wants anyone to suffer just for the sake of it. Nevertheless if, even in our sufferings, we rejoice in him, then he may use them to form in us endurance, strength of character, and a more profound relationship with himself.[3]

Further Reading:

A Grief Observed C.S.Lewis (Faber)
C.S.Lewis lost the wife he loved when she died in great pain because of cancer. In the time which followed he jotted down these thoughts.

Margaret J.Davidson Ross (Hodder)
A teenage girl, dying of cancer, became a source of inspiration through her faith in Christ.

Tortured for Christ R.Wurmbrand (Hodder)
Christians like Pastor Wurmbrand have undergone torture because of their faith, and yet found strength and joy in Christ.

Notes for Section 17

1. John 11.35.
2. Isaiah 63.9; also chapters 42, 49, 50, 52 and 53.
3. Romans 5.1-5; Romans 8.17-30; 1 Peter 2.19-25.

DOESN'T THE BIBLE SHOW A MORAL INCONSISTENCY BETWEEN THE GOD OF WRATH IN THE OLD TESTAMENT AND THE GOD OF LOVE IN THE NEW?

This sort of question may arise in our minds if we have not taken careful account of what the Bible teaches about its own inspiration:

(a) The Bible is not a book of magic incantations. God overruled and inspired the recording of it all, but not everything recorded in it is inspired. Thus the *recording* of what was said by Job's comforters was inspired, but what they *said* certainly was not[1]. Moreover when the Bible records the saying: 'There is no God'[2] it is the act of recording, and not the saying itself, which is inspired.

(b) The Bible is not a textbook of absolute axioms. It is rather one in which the living God meets living people in different ways according to their historical and moral conditions. For example, the Law of Moses permitted divorce, but Jesus said that this had never been God's ideal or absolute will but had been included in the revealed Law of God because the people were hard of heart.[3] Of course, there *are* some absolute axioms, repeated right throughout the Bible, for example that it is wrong to covet.[4] But we must not take it that everything in the Bible is necessarily of this nature.

(c) Statements made by God, if taken in isolation from their whole context, could sometimes be misunderstood. When, for instance, God told Abraham to sacrifice his son, he never really intended this to be done. It *was* a genuine word of God to Abraham, but it would have been quite wrong to use this to build up a doctrine of human sacrifice.

The complete story shows how the testing and strengthening of Abraham's faith was the real intention here.[5]

(d) The complete revelation of God's mind is not encompassed in every section of the Bible. There is rather, throughout the history of the Jews, a building up of the picture of God. The final and full revelation of God came in his Son Jesus Christ[6]. Jesus quoted with approval the Old Testament commandment 'You shall not murder.'[7] But then he deepened it by adding: 'But I say to you, whoever is angry with his brother must stand his trial.' This is just one small example of how the full revelation which was in Jesus deepened and extended what had already been built up.

(e) The Bible is not a Western textbook of either history or science. It is a Middle Eastern book intended to teach us the significance of history and the Personality behind all scientific laws. It is little concerned with matters of exact chronology or of scientific causality (see sections 8 and 10). Thus, for example, when Matthew repeats[8] the genealogies from 1 Chronicles 3.10-19 he omits several of the names. This is in keeping with ancient Hebrew convention, which is more concerned with style, significance, and making things easy to remember than with punctiliously recording every detail.

If we bear these points in mind as we approach the Bible, we shall be helped to understand the problems which arise.

One of the charges frequently made against the Bible is that the Old Testament presents us with a God of wrath while the New Testament depicts a God of love. This charge as it stands, is unfounded, for Jesus himself says that the Law of the Old Testament may be summed up in its commandments to love God and love others.[9] Moreover, he points out that God had, through the prophets, continually cried out for love and mercy rather than sacrifice and ceremony.[10] On the other hand he himself often warned his hearers of 'hell-fire'. Nevertheless it *is* true that the New Testament in general places a greater emphasis on love than does the Old. There would seem to be two main reasons for this:

(i) In the cross of Christ God showed at one and the same time his immense love for us and the severity with which sin must be judged. Before this demonstration there was a danger that his love and forebearance might have been mistaken for softness or indifference to sin. If God really *is* Love, then this would have been intolerable. How could he leave people unaware that their sin was destroying them? Thus we find an emphasis in the Old Testament on the judgement of sin.

(ii) In the nations which surround Israel, even enlightened ones such as the Greeks and Romans, religion and personal ethics were seldom connected. The gods may have been interested in state affairs, in taboos, or in destroying some man who had become too proud; yet they were thought indifferent to perversion, greed and cruelty. Thus Israel was continually tempted to take a similar attitude, and it was in order to save them from doing so that God emphasized the judgement of sin. He wanted to make it quite clear that he *was* interested in our personal ethics, especially in our conduct towards others.

It was God's justice in judging sin which formed the basis for social justice in Israel. The fairness and enlightenment of the legal code given to the Jews far exceed that of almost any other before the present century. In any trial the accused was innocent until proven guilty upon the evidence of at least two witnesses.[11] The death penalty was in use, but for crimes like stealing and assault the principle of restitution was applied.[12] Torture was never allowed. Corporal punishment was carefully restricted, so that the person who had committed the crime would never be despised *as a person;*[13] God was concerned that in any circumstances the value of the individual be remembered. The only punishment which could involve maiming was the 'disfigurement for disfigurement' principle, when one person wilfully injured another.[14] This, like the death penalty, should perhaps be considered more as a deterrent than as merely a punishment.[15] Its deterrent effect was in keeping with the purpose of the death penalty, which was to 'purge evil from among them'.[16] Moreover, not all killing carried the death penalty, but only murder which was planned out of hatred.[17]

It is true that slavery was permitted, but unlike slaves in most other societies, those in Israel had rights. The law concerning sabbaths, for example, extended to cover everyone, so this ensured that slaves too had their days of rest.[18] A Hebrew slave must be freed after seven years.[19] A master was punished for killing *any* slave,[20] and if he gave the slave even so slight an injury as a tooth knocked out, then the slave must go free.[21] A female slave was protected from sexual abuse.[22] Runaways should be given aid.[23] One may compare these safeguards with the absolute power of masters in other societies of that time, or for that matter in later Athens and Rome. And even with these humane safeguards it seems to be implied that, like divorce (see point *(b)*), slavery was not God's ideal. How could it survive if people really loved their neighbours?[24] They were expressly instructed to love the 'strangers and sojourners' and this is what slaves usually were.[25]

As we have tried to explain, a part of the Law taken in isolation may not necessarily reveal either God's complete mind or his ideal (see points *(b)* and *(d)* above). God was dealing with Israel, a people surrounded by nations in which barbarity and cruelty were practised. The fact that, in order to meet their situation, certain laws were less than ideal is far less remarkable than that in the prevailing circumstances such enlightened legislation should exist at all. Could we imagine a heathen king (or indeed a modern Government) having to go to the trouble of arranging false witnesses for a legal trial, in order to seize a piece of property from a commoner? Yet such a case occurred in Israel.[26] In the law of Moses even animals like cows, oxen, goats and birds had rights![27] Social and humanitarian legislation was centuries ahead of its time. Perhaps in some ways it was ahead of ours! For example, the legislation against oppression of the poor even included measures against *economic* oppression.[28] The Lord was always concerned for the underprivileged. He says: *You shall not wrong a stranger or oppress him . . . You shall not afflict any widow or orphan. If you do afflict them, and they cry out to me, I will surely hear their cry; and my wrath will burn, and I will kill you with the sword . . . If you lend money to any of my people with you who is poor, you shall not be to him as creditor, and you shall not extract interest from him.*[29]

We may thus understand why the prophets and psalmists did not necessarily seem afraid of God's wrath and justice, but often called out for it to come. Only God's intervention in justice, it seemed to them, would curb the wickedness of the oppressor. It is with this background of God's concern for human justice that we can better understand the psalmists' strong reaction when they call for the judgement of the wicked. We ourselves feel a quite proper indignation and anger when we see atrocities like those which took place in Belsen and Auschwitz concentration camps. The psalmists felt a similar anger against the evil oppressors of their day. Indeed, if a man did not so react, then there would be something lacking in his moral sense. The Christian way of expressing this anger is in a love for one's enemies and a desire that they should repent. The same attitude is shown in the Old Testament when God says: *Have I any pleasure in the death of the wicked, and not rather that he should turn from his way and live?*[30] Nevertheless the Old Testament psalmists *did* live in a time and situation before the final and full revelation of God in Jesus Christ (see point *(d)*). They had not seen the way in which Christ himself perfectly fulfilled the command to love one's enemies, nor experienced the power of Christ to enable Christians to follow his example. Thus the psalmists sometimes express their quite proper anger and indignation in a pre-Christian way. They do not express God's ideal, nor is their expression valid and binding for all time. God is dealing with them in their own situation and time, and the inspired record gives an accurate picture of how God is encountering them in their lives. In fact, it is probably only through this encounter that the psalmists had their highly developed sense of God's justice between men, and of the value of personality. With this sense came their strong feelings about injustice; this brought with it the temptation to fall into a vindictive spirit, in a way unknown to men unconcerned with such things.

Something which we find difficult to understand is how a God of love could command Israel to destroy and annihilate whole cities, in particular those of the Canaanites. It would be rash to claim to know the complete answer to this difficulty, but we should at least look at the problem in the whole context of God's purposes for mankind, for if taken in isolation, these commands of God might easily be misunderstood (see point *(c)*).

One of the purposes of God in history is that all mankind

should be blessed. A Saviour of the world was sent so that this purpose might be fulfilled. If we think about this we soon realize that it would have been difficult to accomplish this without preparation. When Jesus came, the nation of Israel had already a body of revelation about God's character and purposes. Some Israelites were, moreover, scattered throughout the world as a bridgehead for the spread of the Gospel of Christ. God had achieved this by specially forming their nation out of the descendants of one man, and by letting them know from their very beginning that they were his special people. This man, as we know, was Abraham. To him God revealed his plan to 'bless all the nations of the earth in his descendants'.[31] Connected with the plan was the promise to Abraham that his descendants would possess the land in which he dwelt.[32] Also dwelling in the land were other groups, and their eventual destruction was first predicted to Abraham. Why should such a drastic measure prove necessary? The Bible explains that it was in order to prevent the Israelites from adopting the atrocities, such as child sacrifice, which the Canaanites practised.[33] At the time of Abraham God explained that only after four generations had passed would the evil of the people have become such as to necessitate their destruction.[34] Only then would they constitute a danger to the whole plan of salvation of mankind. Yet this *was* certainly a drastic measure. It was like that of a surgeon who amputates a limb in order to save life. The whole plan for the salvation of the body of humanity was at stake, and surgery was necessary. Later, after Christ fulfilled the central part of the plan, it was not. Rather, those with Christ in their hearts could move out into society to act as a medicine, or in Jesus' terms, as salt [35]. In the situation today, the Christian era, God uses this method.

Yet in all of this God is none the less mindful of the personhood and value of the individuals involved. He told Abraham that the Canaanites would not reach such a level of evil and degradation as to be an insufferable threat to humanity for another 400 years. In Sodom and Gomorrah however, this point had already been reached, and the Lord would destroy them. Yet see to what lengths he was prepared to go, in order to save any righteous people who lived there.[36] We may surely assume that any righteous

Canaanites would be rescued in the same way.[37] At one time, moreover, a declaration of impending destruction was made concerning the city of Nineveh, just as with Sodom and Gomorrah.[38] No escape was offered. Yet, when they repented, *God repented of the evil that he would have done to them, and did it not.*[39] Jeremiah explains that this principle applies to any nation which the Lord declares he is about to pluck up, break down and destroy. If they repent, then he will not bring this judgement on them.[40] In no case was there any torture involved, whether in the destruction of Sodom or of the Canaanites. Their fate may indeed seem terrible to us today, but we must remember that death is not an ultimate evil. Jesus said that some of the chosen people of Israel were in worse case than those of Sodom.[41] Ultimately it is what happens to us in the final assize which is of importance, and this is a result solely of our own attitudes, not of our national destiny or anything else.

In summary: The God of the Bible is a living person and deals with us personally according to our different real-life situations. This may lead to different emphases at different times, but it may be seen that God is unchanged in his attitude of real love to mankind. The Old and the New Testaments, if read in the way they were intended, both show the same God.

Further Reading:

Difficulties in the Bible R.A.Torrey (Moody Press)
Except for a very few passages one would not be aware that this thoughtful book was written over fifty years ago. It contains short sections about a number of difficulties.

Notes for Section 18

1. Job 42.7.

2. Psalm 53.1.

3. Mark 10.2-9.

4. Exodus 20.17; Deuteronomy 5.21; Psalm 10.3; Jeremiah 6.13; Ezekiel 33.31; Mark 7.22; Luke 12.15; Romans 13.9.

5. Genesis 22.1-14, see especially verse 1 which shows that God's intention was to test (not *tempt* as A.V.) the faith of Abraham; he did not intend to receive human sacrifice.

6. Hebrews 1.1-2 et seq.
7. Matthew 5.21, J.B.Phillips.
8. Matthew 1.6-11.
9. Matthew 22.37-40; compare Romans 13.8-10.
10. Matthew 9.13; 12.7, quoting Hosea 6.6.
11. Numbers 35.30; Deuteronomy 17.6; 19.15.
12. Exodus 22.1,4-6,14-17; Leviticus 6.1-7; 24.18.
13. Deuteronomy 25.3.
14. Leviticus 24.19.
15. Deuteronomy 19.20; 21.21.
16. Deuteronomy 17.7; 22.22,24.
17. Numbers 35.1-21.
18. Exodus 20.10; Leviticus 24.22; Numbers 15.16; Deuteronomy 5.14.
19. Exodus 21.1-6; Deuteronomy 15.12.
20. Exodus 21.20,21.
21. Exodus 21.26,27.
22. Deuteronomy 21.10-14.
23. Deuteronomy 23.15.
24. Leviticus 19.17-18.
25. Leviticus 19.33,34; Deuteronomy 10.19.
26. 1 Kings 21.
27. Exodus 23.19; Leviticus 27.28; Deuteronomy 25.4; 22.6,7.
28. e.g. Deuteronomy 23.24-25; 24.12-16, 19-22. Leviticus 25.8-17, 35-38.
29. Exodus 22.21-25.
30. Ezekiel 18.23, 32; 33.11.
31. Genesis 12.1-3.
32. Genesis 12.7.
33. Leviticus 20.1-5; 1 Kings 11.7; 2 Kings 23.10.
34. Genesis 15.16.
35. Matthew 5.13; Mark 9.50; Luke 14.34.
36. Genesis 19.12-16.
37. Is Rahab (Joshua 2.8-14; Hebrews 11.31) a case in point?
38. Jonah 3.4.
39. Jonah 3.10.

40. Jeremiah 18.
41. Matthew 11.24.

DOESN'T THE BIBLE SHOW AN UNHEALTHY PREOCCUPATION WITH BLOOD AND SACRIFICE?

19

Some people feel that the Bible has an unhealthy preoccupation with blood and death. "In the Old Testament," they say, "there is much about animal sacrifice and ceremonies involving blood. In the New Testament there is an emphasis on the cross and blood of Jesus. How are we to accept such primitive ideas in this modern day and age?"[1]

It is interesting to see how much our attitudes are affected merely by the use of words. In English the words *sacrifice* and *kill* have quite different connotations, yet they may be translations of the same Hebrew word.[2] To the Hebrews the killing of animals for food was almost indistinguishable from sacrifice.[3] Such animals, moreover, were killed by methods at least as humane as those used in most of our modern slaughterhouses. Thus it is difficult to see how anyone could find the Hebrews any less humane than ourselves today. As to the emphasis on the blood, to them this was simply a symbol of the life of the animal which was given up in death.[4] Pagan ceremonies of drinking sacrificial blood were totally abhorrent to them, and the respect for the blood and its dedication to God reflected a view that life was sacred and belonged to him. Sacrifices, therefore, cannot be criticised on the grounds that they were cruel.

A few people, however, have felt that all this concerns the ugly and unseemly side of life—surely religion should be concerned with higher and more beautiful things? Yet we see that in our world today the savage reality is all too apparent. There have been two global wars during this century. More recently, there have been conflicts and famines in Africa and Asia. If God is to speak to a violent and bloody world then he must surely speak in a way which is relevant to its problems. God speaks to a violent mankind through a man Jesus Christ, who was himself a focus for undeserved hatred and violence. There is a beauty in this message if it is seen in the context of our violent world, but it is not the beauty of escapism and sentimental idealism. We may see, then, that many of the objections to sacrifice and the cross of Christ are simply emotional or escapist ones.

There does, however, still remain the basic moral question of why the cross was necessary. Jesus clearly taught that one of his main purposes in coming was to die.[5] Why was this? Some have sought to eliminate any moral problem by suggesting that he only died in order to demonstrate God's love. Not only is this difficult to reconcile with many of Jesus' own sayings[6] but it also suffers from a conceptual problem. As I.H.Marshall says: 'A demonstration of God's love must have some point and purpose. To use a familiar illustration: If I am walking on a pier with a friend who jumps into the water and then declares that he has done this in order to show that he loves me, I shall not be impressed. If, however, I am in the water and in danger of drowning, then his act would take on meaning, since it would have the purpose of rescuing me from death. Unless the work of Jesus is somehow related to my need, then it cannot be a true demonstration of love.'[7] The cross of Christ is, of course, a great revelation of God's love[8] but the message of Christ and his apostles clearly assumed that his death also met some real need in man. All the New Testament writers agree that the death of Jesus had something to do with man's sin. The Bible uses several analogies and descriptions to explain what Calvary accomplished. We should, however, take no metaphor too literally or too far in our attempts to understand, for this event was unique and without human parallel. We should not, moreover, be surprised if we fail to grasp its meaning completely. Yet, having said this, we must nevertheless still try to understand the cross as fully as we can.

Something which New Testament writers associate with Christ's death on the cross is the removal of the wrath of God consequent upon sin. Whatever else we are to believe about this, we must be clear that it does not imply a controversy between a loving Son and a wrathful Father. There was no change in attitude on God's part because of Christ's death.[9] On the contrary it was *God* who put forward Christ to be an expiation.[10] It was *God* who was *in Christ* reconciling the world to himself[11] for in him dwelt the fulness of the Godhead.[12] It does not say that God changed his attitude to the world because of Christ's death, but that through it the world was reconciled to him. God loved the world and therefore sent his Son to die for it[13] and it is in this act that the love of *God* is commended to us.[14] We may therefore be certain that God has always loved man. Some have gone further and suggested that the 'wrath of God' is something almost impersonal and operates as an effect of sin.[15] There is an element of truth in this, but as Leon Morris says: 'If God really made the universe a moral universe in which punishment follows sin, then he cannot be exempted from responsibility when it does so.'[16] Just as God operates personally in the process by which flowers are formed[17] so he is surely personally involved in the consequences of sin in his universe. It is valid, therefore, to translate the Bible's description of Christ's death either as 'expiating' sin (R.S.V., N.E.B.) or as 'propitiating' God's wrath (A.V., Phillips).[18] A human being looking as the atrocities of Belsen may feel an emotion somewhat akin to the wrath felt towards sin by a holy and loving God. God, like Christ, loves those at enmity with him[19] and this love is not incompatible with wrath.[20] Indifference or indulgence would be incompatible with love, but wrath is (even in human terms) a consequence of wickedness in a loved one. The New Testament teaches that each time we sin, we arouse God's wrath, and actually store up wrath for a day of judgement.[21] God does not immediately destroy us in judgement but (as it were) holds back the cosmic consequences of our sin. The apostle Paul explains how there would be a moral problem if God were simply delaying an inevitable result of sin.[22] However, in the historic death of Christ the consequences of sin were exhausted.[23] A way was thus made for a person to be right before a moral creator.

How exactly are we to understand what is involved in the wrath which is the consequence of sin? Since our understanding in inevitably limited by our finite natures, it might be best to start by discovering how this wrath works in our own human experience.[24] A way to do this would be to imagine ourselves in a situation where the consequence of our sin has been to damage a human relationship. Let us put ourselves in the position of a profligate wife returning in repentance to her true husband. She has realized that in leaving her family for temporary physical gratification she has broken a worthwhile relationship. Now she returns in sorrow and shame to the husband who loves her. If we discover the reaction she would hope for in her husband, then we may be able to see more clearly what we would hope to find in God if we turn to him in repentance.

Firstly she would be surprised and hurt if she found that he was indifferent to the whole matter. If there had been any value in the relationship, then surely it must have meant something to him that she had run away. She would not be satisfied if he remarked casually: 'Never mind, as long as you were enjoying yourself.' A relationship of value cannot be founded on indifference, and Calvary shows us that God is not indifferent to our sin.

Secondly, the wife would want to hear from his own lips that she is restored to a right relationship with her husband. This, in Biblical language, is what God does when he 'justifies' us. The word means that he declares us to be in a right relationship with himself. Leon Morris has demonstrated the important fact that to the Hebrews the words *justify* and *righteous* were religious terms and not ethical ones.[25] So what is meant by a *righteous* man is one who is in a right relationship with God, and *not* necessarily one who has never done wrong.[26] Thus God *justifies the ungodly.*[27] This does not mean that he says they are good when they are not; it means that he declares them to be in a right relationship with himself—whatever their faults! Yet God must still demonstrate that he takes justice and the condemnation of sin seriously. It is in the cross that he *sets forth* a solution to sin which *declares* how he can pronounce someone right with himself and yet still take the condemnation of sin seriously.[28] In the analogy which we have developed, it will be of little use for the husband to declare his erring wife to be ethically perfect when she herself knows very well that she is not! What she needs is to be restored to a right relationship and yet be sure that he takes her sins seriously. God has accomplished a similar thing for us in his declaration in the cross.

If she has truly repented, then the wife in our analogy will still have a feeling of guilt. She will want to be sure that her husband really understands the depths to which she has sunk. Suppose that he simply refuses to discuss it. His wife may then have to live in fear that he has not fully appreciated the situation and that one day it will be revealed just how bad she had been. This may cause a rift between them. She will always be afraid that something may be said or done which will reveal her past. Such guilt leads to a life of fear and can only be removed by the knowledge that her husband has truly understood everything and yet accepts her. He must have somehow put himself in her place, and understood from the inside the depths of her sin. The experiences of a wife living in fear of discovery are similar to the experiences of some misled religious people. The apostle Paul, for example, was formerly a Pharisee who kept all the points of the Law with great enthusiasm.[29] Yet he regarded it as a bondage from which he needed deliverance.[30] His life was a constant struggle to live up to the law's demands, for example, the command that he should not covet.[31] One lapse in willpower would reveal just how bad he was inside. To know God's standards of perfection seemed only to make all the more serious the effects which sin had in his body and in his psychology.[32] The Law gives a power and meaning to sin, making such a person afraid of death because he fears judgement.[33] He is like the repentant profligate of our analogy because he fears that one day his true nature will be discovered. When this happens then surely God will judge him? It was a tremendous liberation for Paul to discover that God could fully recognize how bad he was, and yet accept him because of his faith.[34] In the cross, God himself was so identified with the sinner[35] that he died for sin. Paul could see in this that God both understood the terrible nature of sin and yet accepted him. Only on this basis could a relationship be set up which involved love, instead of a constant fear of being exposed. The blood which represents Christ's death is pictured as cleansing the conscience of the sinner from his former constant worry about whether he was good enough, and setting him in a relationship with the living God.[36] John adds that perfect love casts out fear, for fear has to do with punishment.[37]

God has involved himself with us and identified himself with us. This, of course, necessitated a certain sacrifice and cost on his part. The husband who receives back his repentant wife has to pay a price in seeking to understand her sin and identify with her. It is no light matter, for it will cost him a great deal. We are here beginning to consider the meaning of the cross to God as well as to ourselves, and so may find it much more difficult to understand what is involved. But it was costly to a holy God to become thus identified with sinful man, and the price is beyond our imagination. The Bible talks of redeeming us, and paying a ransom for us. The word 'redeem' is not simply another word for deliverance, for a price is always implied. When God is described as *redeeming* there is usually a strong effort involved. Morris demonstrates this, and explains: 'This stress on Yahweh's[38] effort seems to be the reason for applying the redemption terminology to his dealings. The effort is regarded as the "price" which gives point to the metaphor. Yahweh's action is at cost to Himself. While he could, so to speak, cope with the situation with a small expenditure of effort, yet because he loves his people he "hath made bare his holy arm in the eyes of all the nations" (Is.52.10).'[39] Mankind is redeemed from the power of sin, death and evil forces, and the price paid is the expenditure of energy within God himself. Divine power and energy were used as Christ on Calvary fulfilled and exhausted in himself the judgement consequences of sin.

Christ is called the *last Adam*[40] for in him the old humanity with all its failings was somehow mystically gathered up and crucified. Thus his death is also our death.[41] The Bible does not say that he was crucified on our behalf as a merely external substitute, for he was fully involved with us. We ourselves were crucified with him and in him. Though we may find it impossible to understand, we died with Christ. Yet, though his objective death was our death, his subjective experience of that death was not our experience. Christ, our substitute, experienced the sufferings for sin, and as a result of his action we do not have to experience them. Thus the consequences of sin (which are death and God-forsakenness) were worked out in him. Yet

Christ was Divine and perfect, and death could not hold him.[42] In rising again from the dead he defeated the spiritual rebels against God who wished to keep man in bondage and fear and death.[43] There is a whole realm of spiritual forces here of which we can know little. In addition to this, God's declaration that we are in a right relationship with him is connected with the resurrection as well as with the death of Christ. He was raised for our justification[44] and our life is bound up with the life he now lives before God.[45] The positive statement of God that sinners can be in a right relationship with him is connected with the resurrection of the one who bore their sins. We are, therefore, included in Christ in the whole process of his death, resurrection and present life. God used this means to bring us into an at-one-ment with himself. This is the meaning of the atonement.

It would be impossible to give in a book such as this an exhaustive theological enquiry into the meaning of the cross. Even were this possible, the limited nature of the human mind will always prevent such an enquiry from being complete.[46] Nevertheless we hope that the above few comments sufficiently show that the cross of Christ need not involve anything morally repugnant nor inconsistent with the Divine love.

Further Reading:

The Work of Christ I.H.Marshall (Paternoster)
The meaning of Christ's death on the cross is outlined within its context of the whole work of Christ in time and in eternity.

The Apostolic Preaching of the Cross Leon Morris (Tyndale)
This scholarly book is not light reading, but it contains much study material for those who wish to examine the subject in detail.

Notes for Section 19

1. Objections to this kind have been made ever since the Christian Gospel was first preached. In the first century the religious people found the cross offensive, and the abstract philosophers found it foolish (1 Corinthians 1.23). It must, moreover, have been an unpopular message to preach to the Romans, to whom crucifixion was for slaves and criminals. Paul nevertheless

affirms that the cross is a power in the lives of those who trust God (1 Corinthians 1.24).
A recent expression of an ancient objection comes from the popular singer and poet Leonard Cohen. He expresses aversion to what he seems to think is Christian belief, in a poem in which the first verse reads:

> I came upon a butcher, he was slaughtering a lamb;
> I accused him there with his tortured lamb;
> He said, "Listen to me, child, I am what I am;
> And you, you are my only son."
>
> (1969 Stranger Music Inc.)

2. The Hebrew word is *zabach* (see 1 Samuel 28.24; Exodus 34.3). The Greek word *thusia* has a similar double meaning (see Luke 15.23; Acts 10.13). In both cases there are, of course, other words also translated 'kill'.

3. See for example: 1 Samuel 9.12-13; 1 Kings 3.15; 1 Kings 8.64-65 where the *feast* was first *sacrificed*. Nearly all sacrifices were eaten, and the killing and eating of animals was usually regarded as having religious significance—see for example Deuteronomy 12, especially verses 17-18 and 21.

4. See chapter 3 of *The Apostolic Preaching of the Cross* by Leon Morris.

5. e.g. Luke 9.22,44; 17.25; 22.19,37; 24.26; John 3.14; 12.32-33; 18.32.

6. e.g. Matthew 20.28; Mark 10.45; John 6 especially verse 51; John 10.15; 15.13.

7. *The Work of Christ* p.75.

8. John 15.13.

9. Theologians of varying viewpoints have shown this. Compare for instance D.M.Baillie in *God Was In Christ* p.186:
'Throughout the whole of this New Testament material there is no trace of any contrast between the wrath of God and the love of Christ, or of the idea that God's attitude to sinners had to be changed by the sacrifice of Christ from wrath and justice to love and mercy.' Leon Morris in *The Apostolic Preaching of the Cross* p.247: 'Even to say that Christ reconciled God does not give us the true picture, for it suggests a disharmony in the Godhead and also raises a doubt as to the constancy of God's love. But we must insist that God's love for us remained unchanged throughout the process of reconciliation.'
P.T.Forsyth draws a distinction between a 'change of feeling and a change of treatment', and he goes on to say, 'God's feeling towards us never needed to be changed. But God's treatment of us, God's practical relation to us—that had to change'.

10. Romans 3.25.

11. 2 Corinthians 5.19-20, also Colossians 1.20.
12. Colossians 1.19; 2.9.
13. John 3.16.
14. Romans 5.8.
15. See C.H.Dodd's Moffat Commentary on Romans (now also published in Fontana).
16. *The Apostolic Preaching of the Cross* p.224. See also chap.5.
17. Matthew 6.28-30.
18. Romans 3.25; 1 John 2.2 and 4.10.
19. Matthew 5.43-48 also Romans 5.8,10.
20. The two theologians already quoted in this section both make this point forcibly. Baillie writes: 'His wrath must not be regarded as something which had to be 'propitiated' and so changed into love and mercy, but rather as being identical with the consuming fire of inexorable divine love in relation to our sins.' (p.189). Morris writes: 'We are not forced to choose between a God of wrath and a God who loves; rather, the wrath is the obverse side of the love. E.H. Gifford has an apposite remark, "Human love here offers a true analogy: the more a father loves his son, the more he hates *in him* the drunkard, the liar, or the traitor".' (p.224).
21. Romans 2.5.
22. Romans 3.24-25.
23. I.H.Marshall uses this phrase in *The Work of Christ*.
24. John 3.36; Romans 1.18.
25. *The Apostolic Preaching of the Cross* p.260ff.
26. For example, Noah in Genesis 6.9 and Lot in 2 Peter 2.7-8 are both declared to be righteous, though both have obvious faults (Genesis 9.21; Genesis 19). This does *not*, of course, mean that God is uninterested in a man's personal ethics, or that his relationship with him is independent of these. It *does* mean that right relationship with God is not the result of moral perfection.
27. Romans 4.5.
28. Romans 3.26.
29. Philippians 3.5-6.
30. Galatians 4, especially verse 5.
31. Romans 7.7.
32. Romans 4.18; 7.5.
33. Hebrews 2.15; 1 Corinthians 15.56.

34. This is an impression one receives from reading Paul's epistles as a whole, rather than from any particular verse, but see Galatians 5.1-13; 1 Timothy 1.15-16.

35. Hebrews 1.16-18; 2 Corinthians 5.21.

36. Hebrews 9.14; 10.2,22.

37. 1 John 4.18.

38. *Yahweh* is the Hebrew word for God.

39. *The Apostolic Preaching of the Cross* p.22.

40. 1 Corinthians 15.45.

41. Romans 6.6-10.

42. Acts 2.24.

43. Colossians 1.15; Hebrews 2.14-15.

44. Romans 4.25.

45. Colossians 13.4; Romans 6.9.

46. Let us remember that the limitations of our minds also prevent us from visualizing many scientific phenomena, for example in the sub-atomic world. We do not assume that this necessarily implies any contradiction in nature!

IF GOD LOVES EVERYONE THEN WHAT HAPPENS TO THOSE WHO HAVE NEVER HEARD?

20 Jesus plainly said that no one comes to the Father except through him[1]. The basis of forgiveness and eternal life for any man must be the atonement made by Christ. We do not pretend to understand completely this atonement, but its importance in the teachings of Jesus is beyond doubt.

Many Christians take Jesus' words to imply that anyone who has not heard of and accepted him will be damned. But what of the many Jews before the birth of Jesus of Nazareth, who had never heard of him and yet were in a right relationship with God? What of Enoch, who *walked with God* years before God's special promises to Abraham and the Jews?[2] The answer seems to be that *any* who have faith in God are accepted by him on the basis of the faithfulness of Christ in his atoning death. The results of

Christ's death gave a whole new dimension of possibility—
not in time but in eternity. Christ, who is sometimes called
'the Word', was in the world although not recognized by
name before his incarnation as a man.[3] Justin Martyr
(c. A.D.100-165) expanded on this theme, and a later
exponent was Clement of Alexandria (c. A.D. 200). It would
seem that some people have been seeking after Jesus Christ
without ever hearing of him. The early chapters of St Paul's
epistle to the Romans talk of the two streams of humanity,
and in chapter two he promises eternal life to those who
seek *glory and honour* and *incorruption*.[4] Elsewhere, Jesus
Christ is revealed as the man crowned with *glory and honour*
(Hebrews 2.7 quoting Psalm 8) who did not see *corruption*
(Acts 2.27 quoting Psalm 16; note that in all these
references it is Christ as *representative man*.) The whole aim
of this section of Romans is to demonstrate that as far as
salvation is concerned the Jews and the Gentiles are on an
equal footing. One might therefore deduce that Gentiles as
well as Jews could be saved through the death of one of
whom they have never heard. Jesus was surely thinking of
some of these when he spoke of 'sheep of another fold' who
did not know him but were already his.[5] John adds that the
very purpose of Christ's death was that these children of
God from every nation should be gathered into one.[6] God's
purpose is always to lead to Christ those who are willing to
learn from him.[7] Surely then, these children of God from
other nations could be led by the Father whom they dimly
recognize, to an eventual fulfilment in Christ of the glory
and honour and incorruption which they seek?

It is true that the Bible never gathers all these hints and
teachings into one plain statement that someone outside the
Judaeo-Christian revelation could be saved. Nevertheless, the
inference of various practical case histories seems to be that
the 'righteous judge of all the earth' will not leave anyone
totally without opportunity to repent and be forgiven,
merely because of the time and place of his birth. Enoch,
Noah and others seem to have had a direct relationship with
God long before the time of Abraham. Jonah was sent to
proclaim judgement to Assyrian Nineveh and they repented.[8]
Rahab the prostitute had only the vaguest knowledge about
the true God; yet her faith, and the action she took on the
basis of what she did know, are commended.[9] The Syrian

Naaman seems to have been granted peace because of his real faith in the one true God, even in spite of his continuing participation in the ceremonies of a pagan society.[10]

The apostle Paul passed through Athens and saw altars 'to the unknown God' almost certainly set up by the Cretan Epimenides some 500 years before.[11] Then, in a sermon during which at least four people were converted, Paul quoted Epimenides on the nature of God.[12] Is it not possible that this man Epimenides, who was reputed to have purified the Athenian's religion and taught them to sacrifice, knew in some limited way the true God?

Throughout history, missionaries have met men who already had some experience or revelation from God. The famous Christian teacher, Watchman Nee, mentions one such man.[13] Another example is that of 'The Transformed Abbot',[14] a Buddhist monk whose first encounter with a personal God occurred years before the clear message of Christ came to fill a gap he still felt in his experience. It would seem that men such as these, no less than believing Jews before Jesus Christ came, were accepted by God on the basis of the death of Jesus even though his name was unknown to them.

Notes for Section 20

1. John 14.6.
2. Genesis 5.22.
3. John 1.10 etc.
4. Romans 2.7.
5. John 10.16.
6. John 11.52.
7. John 6.45.
8. Jonah 3.5; Matthew 12.41; Luke 11.32.
9. Joshua 2.8-13; Hebrews 11.31; James 2.25.
10. 2 Kings 5.15-19.
11. Acts 17.23. The connection is shown in what Diogenes Laertius says in his *Life of Epimenides*. Plutrarch's *Life of Solon* is also important in showing us Epimenides' opposition to 'cruel and barbarous customs' and emphasis on sacrifices and justice as keys to religious life. For further information see: *Asianic Elements in Greek Civilisation* by Sir W.M. Ramsay (1927) ch.3;

Fragmente der Vorsokratiker by Diels pp.27-36; *Presocratic Philosophers* by Kirk and Raven, pp.20-23, 40-47.

12. Acts 17.28 (see also Titus 1.12) quoting the quatrain:
    They fashioned a tomb for thee, O holy and high one—
    The Cretans, always liars, evil beasts, idle bellies.
    But thou art not dead; thou livest and abidest for ever,
    For in thee we live and move and have our being.

13. *What Shall This Man Do?* p.43 and also *A Table in the Wilderness* passage for September 22nd.

14. by Karl Reichelt (Lutterworth Press).

THEN WHY BOTHER TO PREACH IF ALL RELIGIONS LEAD TO GOD?

21

It is not true to say that all religions lead to God. The Hindu believes that God is in both the good and the evil things, for God is everything. Thus to the Hindu the word 'God' means something totally different from its meaning when used in the Bible. In many branches of Buddhism God has no place at all, and the 'great man' of Confucius is more concerned with burial rites than with God. Thus, since the different religions use the word 'God' to refer to different concepts, how could they all lead to the same person? What we do believe is that in many societies some individuals have sought the true God and have been forgiven by him because of the work of Jesus on the cross. When, in such societies, the Christian 'good news' is proclaimed to them, any who have some limited knowledge of the Father will be led by him to accept Christ Jesus. The same sort of thing applied to Israelites who loved God at the time when Jesus first appeared, and he talks about it in John chapter six. We may be sure, therefore, that if the real revelation of Jesus Christ is presented to anyone today whose heart is right before God, then he will be led to accept Christ as Saviour.

The full revelation of God is in Jesus Christ. To know him is an experience above any other. Many who were right before God were led by him into this further experience in the first century. This was true of Cornelius, who was not a Jew but a 'God-fearer' whose prayers and holy life were acceptable before God and who was guided by him to seek Christ and receive the Holy Spirit. Peter, realizing that he did not need to preach repentance to such a man of prayer, could only remark: 'I perceive that God is no respecter of persons, but in every nation he who fears him and works righteousness is acceptable to him.'[1] Lydia is a similar example[2]. Such people as these knew how to pray and were acceptable to God. Nevertheless the message of Christ was preached to them, for only in Christ would come a real life of sharing with God and understanding of him. This would involve a knowledge of forgiveness, the power to live in God's way, and a purpose and direction in life.

In addition to this, we preach because the Holy Spirit may lead others to repentance through hearing about God's judgement and love as manifested in Jesus Christ. In any society there remain many who are not right with God; he would have us work to enable everyone at least to hear how wonderful and loving God is.

Further Reading:

Religion, Origin and Ideas Robert Brow (Tyndale)
An introductory sketch of the history and leading ideas of world religous thinking. He also considers the question of whether all religions lead to God.

Notes for Section 21

1. Acts 10.34-35.
2. Acts 16.13-14.

EVEN IF EVERYONE SEEMS TO HAVE AN OPPORTUNITY TO BELIEVE, WHAT IS THE POINT OF TORTURING UNBELIEVERS FOR EVER?

22

God does not purposely set out to torture people. The fact is that the universe is so constituted that the evil man is bound to be miserable in the end. Even in this life there is a certain emptiness in the pleasure of the evil man, as the book of Habakkuk points out.[1] If a man rejects God, he rejects Love; he begins then to work out in his own psychology the process of conflict and disintegration. To what can this lead ultimately but misery? It is simply the wages of sin which are death[2] even though God is in this natural process just as much as he is in the natural process by which the sparrows are fed.

Christians do differ over whether hell (Hebrew and Greek: *'Gehenna'*) is a conscious misery for unlimited time[3] or a disintegration which eventually becomes total. Some scholars have pointed out that the Greek word *aionios* which our Bible translates 'eternal' may not refer simply to unlimited time. It refers rather to that which is enduring, yet somehow 'timeless', to the things of the spirit as against those of this fleeting material world.[4] Thus *eternal death* or what John in the Revelation calls *the second death*, may mean the disintegration of what is spiritual as against the disintegration of the physical body which follows physical death. The physical body of someone who had been an *outcast* or *criminal* might be burned on a rubbish dump outside Jerusalem called 'Ge Henna' or 'the Valley of Hinnom'.[5] On this dump the 'worms never died' and the 'flames were never put out' as the remains of dead bodies along with other refuse were continually being consumed.[6] Perhaps then, we are intended to picture the remains of the 'spiritual body' of some 'spiritual *criminal* and *outcast*' as being consumed in *Gehenna* (i.e. the 'Hell' of our versions.)

Thus in Hell their worm does not die and the fire is never quenched.[7] Sometimes it is said that if eternal life goes on for ever then eternal death must be torture for unlimited time. But physical life (in time) is continuous, whereas physical death and disintegration is a process culminating in a conclusion. There is obviously no contradiction in this, and remembering the true meaning of the word eternal we may certainly visualize the relationship between eternal life and eternal death in this way.

Other Biblical references are sometimes cited in attempts to prove conclusively that the Christian doctrine of hell involves conscious suffering for unlimited time; careful examination of Greek terms and the literary background of a passage however always leaves the question open. For example, in the parable of the rich man and Lazarus[8] the text does not refer to *Gehenna* but to *Hades*, which Jews of the period thought of as the temporary place where the spirit awaits the last judgement. The place of *Gehenna* (or the 'lake of fire' as it was also called) was totally separate in Jewish thought, and the rabbis differed as to whether it involved suffering or extinction. Had Jesus intended the word *Hades* to be taken in a sense totally different from the natural contemporary meaning then he would surely have said so. Another example of a text which has been cited to prove that hell is conscious suffering is that in Revelation 14.11 about the smoke of their torment ascending (literally) 'unto ages of ages'; the reader might compare the context in which this same phrase is used in Isaiah chapter 34.

We would finish in similar vein to Dr Alfred Edersheim, one of the great Christian authorities on Jewish thought. He wrote on *eternal punishment*: 'Thus far it has been the sole aim of the present writer to set before the reader, so far as he can, all the elements to be taken into consideration. He has pronounced no definite conclusion, and he neither wishes nor purposes to do so . . . But of these things does he feel fully assured: that we may absolutely trust in the lovingkindness of our God; that the work of Christ is for all and of infinite value, and that its outcome must correspond to its character; and lastly for practical purposes, that in regard to those who have departed (whether or not we know of grace in them) our views and our hopes should be the widest (consistent with Scripture teaching) and that as regards ourselves, personally and individually, our views as to the need of absolute and immediate faith in Christ as Saviour, should be the closest and most rigidly fixed.'

The one thing which is certain is that God wants everyone, including us, to repent,[9] since there is a hell to be saved from.

Further Reading:

The Life and Times of Jesus The Messiah A.Edersheim (Longmans)
A standard work by one of the greatest Christian scholars of Hebrew background and thought. Appendix xix examines the question of eternal punishment.

Two well known evangelicals, Mr Motyer and Dr Atkinson, have written from the two different positions on eternal punishment. We cannot agree with everything in either book, but recommend them as reasonable presentations of their respective viewpoints:
After Death J.A.Motyer (Hodder)
Life and Immortality Basil Atkinson (Phoenix Press, Taunton)

Notes for Section 22

1. Habakkuk 2.4: 'Behold his soul is puffed up, it is not upright in him: but the just shall live by his faith.' (R.V.) Some men, such as Socrates, who were outside of the Biblical revelation, have also understood this point.

2. Romans 6.23.

3. See e.g. the lexicons by Souter or Schleusner.

4. For Biblical uses of this word *aionios* or eternal, see e.g. Jude 6 and 7; Romans 16.25; 2 Timothy 1.9; Revelation 14.6; and the Septuagint Genesis 17.8; Leviticus 16.34; Numbers 25.13; Isaiah 24.5; and Habakkuk 3.6 'The *everlasting* hills melted at his *everlasting* going forth.'

5. See the *New Bible Dictionary*.

6. See Isaiah 66.24.

7. Mark 9.48.

8. Luke 16.20-31.

9. e.g. Ezekiel 18.23; Acts 17.30.

CAN'T I BE GOOD WITHOUT BEING A CHRISTIAN?

23 Of course non-Christians are capable of loving and of doing good. Something, however, which we have not yet found is a person willing to claim that he has *never* done *anything* wrong or unkind. It does seem that in the final analysis our lives and the sort of people we are will have to stand compared to the perfect life of Christ. God is in any case more interested in what we are and become than in the opportunities which may or may not have been given to us to show it. Our motives, rather than merely what we do, may often be a better guide to our character. There is nothing wrong, for example, with our enjoying helping others, but there *is* something wrong when the gaining of such enjoyment becomes our prime motive. In such a case we may even be secretly *glad* that someone has the misfortune to need help.[1] This is a form of self-centredness which often we find difficult to recognize, even in ourselves. A less subtle form of self-love sometimes causes us to do good in order to receive other people's praise. Christians, no less than others, may find such motives in themselves. Some Christians, moreover, give the impression that they are trying to earn, by their good works, a better place for themselves in heaven. A few adopt an unreal humility, ostentatiously attributing all their good works to God.

None of these unfortunate attitudes can alter the fact that a Christian does have a resource for true humility which is not open to an atheist. He may quietly and unobtrusively accept praise and thanks, and in his own heart give the praise to the One who gives him 'strength to love'. In addition the Christian knows that compared with the standard of Jesus Christ he is still far from being truly good. An atheist[2] can ascribe his goodness to no one but himself. He can, moreover, only compare himself with other imperfect men. This is not to say that all atheists and non-Christians consciously do this, but that logically it is the only alternative open to them.

In the practical sphere of well-doing in the right spirit, there seem to us to be areas in which a living faith is vital. In the first place, do we not sometimes find that it is impossible to love someone? In such a situation the Christian may pray for and receive the love which will enable him to continue with right motives. Secondly, in some difficult situations only the wisdom that comes from God seems sufficient. Thirdly, the Christian brings forgiveness and acceptance of the person as he is; but he may go further than that: he may offer him as well the power of God to live more fully and to live more like Christ. Lastly, many people who are in trouble have a deep desire for a meaningful future, a reason for life. This is something which we have never found convincingly presented by an atheist, however good he might be in himself.

We do believe, then, that non-Christians can do good, although the Christian has definite advantages. It seems, however, rather unprofitable to have long intellectual discussion over this question; it surely could not be an obstacle to anyone becoming a Christian. If he indeed wants to do good, then why not accept the resources found in Christ?

Further Reading:

The Four Loves C.S.Lewis (Fontana)
A useful analysis of the different types of relationships which we might call love relationships.

Strength to Love Martin Luther King (Fontana)
Dr King was imprisoned twelve times, had his house bombed twice, was threatened with death hundreds of times, received a near fatal stabbing, and was eventually assassinated. He tells how he found the source of strength to love his enemies.

Notes for Section 23

1. Dr Hillman, the Director of the Carl Jung Institute in Zurich, writes of something similar to this in *Insearch*: 'A counsellor may need to instruct and educate, to teach what he knows, because it fulfils an essential part of himself.'
2. Unless he takes a mechanistic view of man, and denies personhood and freedom of choice.

BUT RELIGIOUS PEOPLE ALWAYS SEEM TO BE CONCERNED WITH SUCH SILLY LITTLE THINGS!

24 They do indeed! The people that Christ really attacked were the religious people (see Matthew chapter 23). He got on very well with the traitors, the prostitutes and the general 'riff-raff', and was himself strongly criticised for this by many of the clergy, theologians, and religious bigots, whose religiosity he condemned and who were eventually to crucify him. They reprimanded his disciples over ceremony[1] and sabbath observance.[2] He called them play-actors and blind leaders of the blind, reminding them that all the prophets had cried out for love and mercy rather than religiosity.[3] The word *religion* is used in the New Testament in only three places, always it seems, with slight distaste: for example, James says that *real* religious practices should be personal purity and acts of love, not ostentatious ceremony and doctrinal verbosity.[4] The apostle Paul spent much of his life fighting against unhealthy preoccupation in some Christians with details of ritual observance.

Jesus told us that we should *know men by their fruits.*[5] Now the fruit of the Spirit is love, joy, peace, patience, kindness, goodness, faithfulness, gentleness, and self-control. But the works of the flesh are immorality, impurity, licentiousness, idolatry, enmity, strife, jealousy, anger, selfishness, dissension, party-spirit, envy, drunkenness, etc., and those who practise such things are no part of God's kingdom.[6] We notice that a correct understanding of all the minor points of doctrine does not seem to be listed as a fruit of the Spirit! So much for knowledge; elsewhere Paul adds that not only knowledge but faith too, and even martyrdom are worthless if we do not have love.[7]

Throughout the long years of carnage, bickering, hypocrisy, enmity and pride in the history of the church, there have always been some men and women with lives set on fire with the love of Christ and exhibiting the Spirit's fruits. Some became famous, but many in all parts of the globe have gone quietly on in obscurity, loving and serving God and their fellow men. It is with such revolutionary faith and love that Christ and his true disciples are concerned.

Further Reading

From among the mass of Christian biography, here are a few varied experiences:

Forgive Them J.E.Church (Hodder)
The story of an African Pastor and martyr.
The Seed Must Die Yoon Choon Ahn (I.V.F.) A Korean Pastor who saved the man who murdered his two sons.
A Prisoner and Yet Corrie Ten Boom (C.L.C.)
The author found Christ a source of strength during her time in Ravensbruch concentration camp.
Black and Free Tom Skinner (Paternoster) An American Negro tells how he found a real freedom in Christ.
The Cross and the Switchblade D.Wilkerson (Spire)
How the Christian Gospel broke into the violent world of teenage gang warfare in Brooklyn.
The Jesus Family in Communist China E.Vaughan Rees (Paternoster) The story of some Christian village communes.
The Bamboo Cross H.E.Dowdy (Hodder)
The transformation through Christ, brought to some primitive tribes in Vietnam.
The Small Woman Alan Burgess (Evans)
The story of Gladys Aylward, the parlourmaid who became a missionary and ran an orphanage in China.
Miracle on the River Kwai Ernest Gordon (Fontana)
How some prisoners in a Japanese P.O.W. camp came to find a reality in Christ.
Angel At Her Shoulder K.E.Wilson (Hodder)
A missionary whose work in Formosa helped hundreds.
God's Underground Richard Wurmbrand (Hodder)
Christian love operating in Rumanian prisons.

Notes for Section 24

1. Mark 7.
2. Mark 2 and 3.
3. Matthew 9.13; 12.7; and chapter 23.
4. James 1.27.
5. Matthew 7.16
6. Galatians 5.19-24.
7. 1 Corinthians 13.

THEN YOU DON'T THINK THAT CHRISTIANITY IS NARROW AND RESTRICTIVE?

25 It is true that sometimes even sincere Christians give the impression that their faith is restrictive. This is not only because they themselves feel that they must abstain from certain things, but because they wish to impose the same prohibitions on others. Some habits which the Bible never prohibits are condemned by them, not merely because these are harmful to health and a waste of money, but because they are thought to be somehow incompatible with clean living. Sadly, it is sometimes the abhorrence of such habits which may become the mark by which such people identify a 'spiritual' Christian. Obviously the New Testament does forbid some things, such as adultery and murder, but no one should add to Christ's commands a series of petty regulations. Jesus himself said that it was dangerous to focus attention on external things and what people consume, for it is the heart that is important.[1] Paul too, taught that the true mark of closeness to Christ concerned personal characteristics such as love, joy, peace, etc.[2] His attitude to such questions as what we eat or drink, was that it was a personal matter and no one should foist regulations on others.[3] Nothing is unclean of itself, but what every Christian *must* do is to discover before God what he wants of him personally.[4]

The Christian, then, is free. Yet Christianity is obviously not unlimited licence, and Christ did talk of a *narrow gate to life*[5]. What did he mean by it? He himself tells us the story of the young man who goes away to assert his freedom and live it up. The trouble is that like so many of our daring and exciting twentieth century liberations it goes sour on him! At length he *comes to himself* and returns home to his father, whereupon they have a home-coming party with music and dancing. There is, he discovers, a place of love, purpose and sharing together which gives a real and

lasting satisfaction. The famous psychiatrist Dr Paul
Tournier writes: 'To be free is to become oneself once
more.' He talks of how we are bound to passions or habits
which have long since ceased to give real pleasure, and of
how we often become tied to a 'mask' or 'personage' which
we have assumed, and find that we must act it out to others.
Freedom is discovering our true person, which also means
ultimately becoming what we were designed for.[6]

But there is another character in Jesus' story. The elder
brother reveals that he has all along *repressed* a desire to
live it up in feasting with his friends.[7] This is the point. The
prodigal son found that licence was not freedom and
returned to find the satisfying discipline of love. The elder
son tried to imitate the actions of a truly free man, and
suppressed his desire for licence. The first represents a
repentant sinner who found what Jesus called life abundant;[8]
the second represents the religious moralist and
authoritarian. It was men of this second type who called
Christ a winebibber and a glutton![9] Later, the apostle Paul
openly opposed any suggestion by such men as these that
rigorous self-imposed regulations could be a path to holiness.
'Why do you submit to regulations: Do not handle, Do not
taste, Do not touch?' This is not, he says, the Christian way
to develop a personality free from selfishness.[10]

Freudian psychology did a great service in spotlighting
the hypocrisy and danger of repression. But the solution
that Freudians once offered was the removal of all
restrictions, and in practice this proved not to lead to the
desired psychological adjustment. Thus, for example, child
psychology based on extreme ideas of self-expression has
fallen increasingly into disrepute.[11]

The answer is neither repression nor moral anarchy, but
true discipline. Dr Tournier comments: 'The only true
source of discipline in the world is fellowship with Christ.
The moment Jesus Christ really comes into a person's life,
he finds a true discipline, one which is no longer rigid,
formalist, or heavy, but joyous, supple, and spontaneous.
Discipline is not the goal of life, nor even a means of
coming to Christ. It is a consequence of the change in
outlook which takes place when Christ breaks into a
person's life[12] . . . it would be a serious misunderstanding of
the wonderful message of Jesus Christ to see the Bible as a

collection of Divine laws to which men ought to try to conform. This would be to fall into the error of legalism, formalism, or moralism. Moral effort of this kind has nothing whatever to do with the miraculous transformation brought about by Christ in the person who opens his heart to him. The Gospel is not a call to effort but to faith.[13] ... Advice acts from without. The spiritual revolution takes place within. When a man encounters Jesus Christ he feels all at once freed from some passion or habit to which he has been enslaved, from some fear or rancour against which he has deployed his stoutest efforts in vain.'[14]

Far from being narrow, the message of Christ invites us to a life lived to the full. It gives to it a meaning and a purpose which agnosticism or apathy cannot offer. It is positive and not negative. Relationship with God provides a ground for full and loving relationships with others.

Further Reading:

The Healing of Persons Paul Tournier (Collins)
Most of this book is about other questions, but there is a considerable amount of material relevant to this section.
Unafraid To Be Ruth Etchells (I.V.P.)
A lecturer in English examines the problem of man's identity as shown in literature, and how he finds his true fulfilment in Christ.
Humanism, Positive and Negative D.M.Mackay (I.V.F.)
This very brief booklet by Professor Mackay indicates ways in which it is humanism rather than Christianity which is negative in approach.

Notes for Section 25

1. Matthew 15.17-20.
2. Galatians 5.19-24, and see also last section.
3. Romans 14.13.   4. Romans 14.14,12.
5. Matthew 7.13.
6. The famous atheist philosopher Albert Camus certainly did not see the world from a Judaeo-Christian viewpoint. Yet he too saw the distinction between licence and freedom, and wrote: 'Absolute domination by the law does not represent liberty, but nor does absolute freedom of choice. Chaos is also a form of servitude. Freedom only exists in a world where what is

possible is defined at the same time as what is not possible. Without law there is no freedom.' *The Rebel* (1951).

7. Luke 15.29-31. 8. John 10.10.
9. Luke 7.34.
10. Colossians 2.20-23 in R.V. or R.S.V. or N.E.B.
11. The third 'best seller' in the world is a book on child care by Dr Spock. In 1969 a new edition was published, and he made it clearer than ever that he in no way advocated the extreme permissive approach.
12. *The Healing of Persons* p.189.
13. *ibid* p.209. 14. *ibid* p.213.

BUT AREN'T CHRISTIANS AFRAID OF SEX EXPERIENCE?

26

The idea that sex is somehow dubious or nasty is unchristian. Eve was created *primarily* as a companion for her husband (and, in spite of some recent religious pronouncements, *not* principally for procreation—see Genesis 2.18) for the two were to become one flesh.[1] At all times the Bible treats such union as sacred and good, and many Bible passages refer figuratively to the church itself as the *bride of Christ.* One whole book of the Bible[2] is a pure love poem, and the language there is certainly in no way inhibited. The apostle Paul is sometimes wrongly accused of prudery, on the basis (so we gather) that in a place where he is careful to distinguish his personal opinion from the word of God, he says that he prefers missionaries to be free from family ties![3] What he, and the New Testament generally, quite properly say is that the sex drive should be channeled into its most emotionally satisfying outlet, namely marriage. To have spiritual and physical union with a lifelong lover who is also a partner is surely more satisfying than anything else. We do not champion the respectable prudery of some repressed religious folks, for Jesus showed more anger over pride and hyprocrisy than over sexual sin.[4] Nevertheless, to stampede to the opposite extreme of moral anarchy seems just as harmful and more irrational. Sometimes a Christian's friends tell him that he should seek some experience or other, such as sex, drugs, or occultism, to avoid being 'narrow'; it will surely mature him, they say. Let us consider some points here:

(a) Suppose, first of all, that one's criterion for living were simply to have as many experiences as possible. What is apparently a choice between whether or not to seek a certain experience may in fact be a choice between two quite different but equally 'valid' experiences. Often these will be *mutually exclusive*. For example one cannot have *both* promiscuous sex *and* the thrill of marrying in purity a lover with whom to grow in lifelong unity. If our criterion is indeed to have as many experiences as possible, then these and other *mutually exclusive* experiences present to us a problem.

(b) Moreover most people, if pressed, would admit that their objective in life is not merely to have a multiplicity of indiscriminate experiences. Their real aim is perhaps *fulfilment* or *happiness*, and they see experience as a means of achieving this end. Now it is quite conceivable that sex or drugs or some other experience might be the best means to this end, but whether or not this is so must surely be decided on some reasonable basis. It cannot, as is frequently the case, merely be assumed. The Christian feels there are good grounds for believing that fulfilment in life is best achieved by enjoying what God has created in the way God intended. If he denies himself certain experiences it is because he believes that something better is available.

One cannot do everything at once, and some experiences can only take place at a considerable time after others. This forces on us the necessity to make some sort of selection. Nor can anyone lightly say: 'You don't know whether you would like anything unless you try it.' A part of being human is that our experiences usually leave some mark, whether significant or otherwise, on our minds. After a visit to a meat pie factory we may be unable to enjoy another meat pie! It may be that God will guide some particular individual into having an experience which is unpleasant, but this is generally designed to stimulate the person into action towards righting some situation through the power of his faith. It is difficult to imagine how experiences such as sexual licence, drug-taking, or occultism could serve such an end, and those who press such experiences upon

Christians seldom claim that this is their motive.

None of this is to deny that many Christians are quite unnecessarily more restrictive in their activities than God intended, but it is certainly to deny that whenever a Christian refuses some experience it must be because he is narrow minded.

Further Reading:

The New Morality Arnold Lunn and Garth Lean (Blandford) A Catholic and an Anglican attack the assumptions behind total permissiveness. Most people, even those of a different viewpoint, find this book thoughtful and stimulating.

Notes for Section 26

1. Genesis 2.24.
2. The Song of Solomon.
3. 1 Corinthians 7.32-35, but see also verse 17, and 1 Timothy 5.14.
4. Compare John 4 and John 8.

WHAT EXACTLY DOES IT MEAN TO BE A CHRISTIAN?

It would be foolish to suggest that atheists could not be good and loving people; but it is simply a confusion of language to call someone a Christian who does not accept the main thrust of the teachings of the historic Christ. To us that main thrust seems to be:

(a) There exists a personal and loving creator God who wants us to freely submit our wills to him, and receive the gift of eternal life.

(b) Jesus was the uniquely complete expression of God, and his death was necessary to link up man and God.

(c) Man has a problem with sin which can only be overcome by God reaching down into his situation, and by him responding in repentance and faith.

(d) Death's power was broken through the resurrection of Jesus from the dead. (See 1 Corinthians 15 for Paul's analysis of why this is central).

(e) The commandments to love God and love other

people are the guiding principle in discipleship of Christ.

We do not imply that to believe these points makes one a Christian. Being a Christian involves having a *relationship* with Jesus Christ. To have a relationship with someone implies a belief that they are alive, but to believe that they are alive does not prove that one knows and loves them.[1] A Christian will believe, or come to believe, all these points, but to believe all these points does not make one a Christian.

In the real relationship of which we speak, the Christian discovers an interchange and communion with God through the medium of prayer, reading the Bible, and meditating on it before God. This true communion with God affects his spirit or inner consciousness, his mind, his will, and from time to time his emotions. In his inner consciousness, God and his love can be known and become increasingly real. In his mind the Christian receives data which give content to his encounter with God, and understanding and ability to express it increases. Likewise does his awareness of his place in the universe increase. His will is thus directed into a life of service and love to God and to his fellow man.

The emotions do play some part in Christian experience but should not be played upon, nor should emotional experiences be sought. One's aim should be to be more like Christ and to exhibit the fruit of the Spirit. A Christian is not perfect but should be seeking to let God show him new areas in his life where repentance and change are necessary. If the sin is honestly confessed with a desire to be different and to make restitution where possible, then God will forgive him and cleanse him from all unrighteousness;[2] he is not now a rebel coming to a king, as he was at his conversion, but a son coming to his father. The Christian life is a day by day adventure of a son sharing in the life, projects, thoughts and purpose of God his Father, and being involved in his movement in history and eternity.

Notes for Section 27

1. See James 2.19.   2. 1 John 1.9.

YOU CHRISTIANS ALWAYS QUOTE THE BIBLE, DO I HAVE TO BELIEVE IT ALL TO BECOME A CHRISTIAN?

28

In the previous section we have explained that to be a Christian is to have a relationship with God and to have the risen Christ as Saviour.[1] One could not say that you *have* to believe in all of the Bible in order to do this. The Jesus to whom we become committed *is* the historical Jesus who is described in the Bible; but this does not necessarily mean that when we come to him we either know or accept all the details in the records. Many of the converts in the early church did not even know about much of what the Old Testament said—and the New Testament was not yet written! One of the present authors became a real Christian some months before he came to accept all of the Bible as inspired.

We have elsewhere explained why we do believe the Bible to be authoritative (section 12) and how one should approach it (section 18). It is obviously of importance to someone who has become a Christian to discover whether or not the Bible is fully reliable, and he will surely begin to ask questions about its authority and how to approach it. Above all, he should ask the God he now serves what *he* thinks of it. These questions rightly concern the new Christian, but they certainly should not deter someone from becoming a Christian. If you find parts of the Bible incredible, this does not prevent you from making the act of committal to Christ outlined in the next section.

Note for Section 28

1. 1 John 5.12.

WHAT WOULD I DO TO BECOME A CHRISTIAN?

29 Jesus gave to all those who received him the power to become the children of God—to all those who believed on his name.[1] But how in practice is one to receive Christ? The simple message proclaimed by the early Christians was: *Repent towards God and believe on the Lord Jesus Christ*, and this supplies the answer.

Repentance

The first essential in repentance towards God is the readiness to be as honest before him and with ourselves as we are able.[2] The second essential is a willingness to follow his plan and purpose for our lives. These two features are common to all who accept God's offer of a relationship with him, but there are many differences. Some may feel that they hardly believe God is really there, others are convinced intellectually but have never experienced the reality in their lives. Many feel very sure that God is there, but feel extremely hesitant about capitulating to his will for them, when it might involve so much. Some see fully how far their own lives fall short of the perfect life lived by Christ, others have little consciousness of the guilt which belongs to the wrongs they know they have done. We must be willing to accept ourselves *as we are*, for we are seeking to begin an individual relationship with God. We must not try to copy others, or expect exactly the same experience to follow. It is with this honesty of mind that we should tell God that from now on we want to go his way. But this alone does not make a Christian.

Faith

A true Christian is one who believes on the Lord Jesus Christ. A sick person is not made well by faith in a doctor, or knowledge about a doctor, but by the doctor himself. Our knowledge about the doctor helps us to go to him. Our confidence in the doctor also helps us to go to him. But the essential point is that we must place ourselves in the doctor's hands. In the same way we may know much or little about Christ, and our confidence in him may be great or small, but the essential point is an *act* of faith whereby we commit ourselves into his hands. It is those who actually *call* on the Lord who are saved.[3] The confidence which Christians rightly have in their Lord may develop after this act of faith.

The Outcome

In the relationship with Christ which has begun, the Christian should begin to read the Bible seriously, starting, we suggest, with the gospel of John. The Bible will become a living book as God speaks to him through it, and prayer will become a time of real communion.

Here there should be a word of warning. Some people find that their experiences during conversion are not as dramatic as they have been led to believe by the stories of conversions which they have been told. They 'feel no different', and no blinding lights from heaven shone! Yet, surprisingly, they find later that when they try to describe what happened they begin to use those same words and phrases which appeared at first too dramatic. It need not be assumed that they are reading anything back into their experience, but a paradox arises simply because language itself is not very adequate for the description of experiences and personal relationships.

The Gospels record an incident which we have found to be helpful to some people during their conversion and first few weeks of Christian experience: 'Then he (Jesus) made the disciples embark and go on ahead to the other side, while he sent the people away; after doing that, he went up the hill-side to pray alone. It grew late, and he was there by himself. The boat was already some furlongs from the shore, battling with a head-wind and a rough sea. Between three and six in the morning he came to them, walking over the lake. When the disciples saw him walking on the lake they were so shaken that they cried out in terror: "It is a ghost!" But at once he spoke to them: "Take heart! It is I; do not be afraid."

'Peter called to him: "Lord, if it is you, tell me to come

to you over the water." "Come", said Jesus. Peter stepped down from the boat, and walked over the water towards Jesus. But when he saw the strength of the gale he was seized with fear; and beginning to sink, he cried, "Save me, Lord." Jesus at once reached out and caught hold of him, and said, "Why did you hesitate? How little faith you have!" They then climbed into the boat; and the wind dropped. And the men in the boat fell at his feet, exclaiming, "Truly you are the Son of God."[4]

Was this ghost-like figure, so far removed from Peter's everyday experience, really Jesus? His doubts only dissolved after he had stepped out, and he could later affirm: *'Truly you are the Son of God.'* He had to act upon what he already knew, and this action was initiated by talking to the indistinct figure: *'Lord, if it is you, tell me to come to you...'* To many, God is a shadowy figure whose very existence may be in doubt. The way to an inner assurance, however, is through action. One begins by actually speaking to God and saying that one wants to come to him.

What were the thoughts that rushed through Peter's mind before he stepped out? Was it really Jesus? What would his friends in the boat think? Suppose it didn't work, and he sank, how foolish he would look! How could he face the storm, raging around them? How many people since then have not come to Christ for fear of what their friends might think, or fear of the storms of persecution that might come, or fear that it might not work?

Peter started out, looking into the face of Jesus Christ. Perhaps he was tempted to look down at his feet to examine the great experience he was having. Had he done so then he would have surely begun to sink, and so lost the experience altogether. Christians too may become so engrossed in examining themselves to see how their experience is developing, that it begins to elude them altogether. If we keep looking towards the face of Jesus, the experience will take care of itself.

Peter saw the strength of the gale and was seized with fear. Sinking, he cried: *'Save me, Lord,'* and was *at once* rescued. God's concern is that we should come, and if we begin to sink in fear, the Lord Jesus Christ will save us if we call to him.[5]

The whole secret is to keep looking towards Jesus Christ

as we meet him day by day and find him in the Gospels.
Leave the laughter of some friends behind us in the boat,
walk through the storm, and let the experience take care of
itself. Finally, a deep peace and joy in believing is left to us
as we know that Jesus has come to be with us and guide
and stimulate us in the adventure of Christian living.

Summary:

To become a Christian a person must begin talking
personally to God who is himself a person:

(1) Confessing his failings and confirming his willingness
to do God's will.

(2) Thanking him for the forgiveness offered through
Christ's work in dying for him.

(3) Asking Christ to enter his life and share it with him.

He will.

Notes for Section 29
1. John 1.12.
2. Luke 8.15.
3. Romans 10.13: 'Whoever shall call on the name of the Lord shall be saved.'
4. Matthew 14.22-33 N.E.B.
5. See note 3.

FOREWORD TO
PROFESSING EXISTENTIALISTS

This special 'foreword' comes at the end because to many
readers it may be of little interest or importance. The issue
dealt with is whether truth is objective and knowable. One
can of course, discuss the truth about Christianity only if
truth itself is real and objective. Probably most people
would assume automatically that it was, but this foreword
is for those who might say something like this:
statement (a) 'Truth is different to different people'.

By this they do not merely mean that people differ over
which things they find important, but that the actual truth
itself differs. Now statement (a) might be reworded: 'It is
true to say that truth is different to different people'. This
then becomes nonsense, since it contains a statement of
objective truth of the type that it denies exists. One might

then try to reformulate it as: 'It is true *to me* that truth is different to different people.' But this fails to resolve the contradiction, since it could be rewritten: 'It is true to say that it is true to me that truth is different to different people.' Once again the statement is self-contradictory.

Wittgenstein found that by his own rules his theory was meaningless, and the professing existentialist has the same problem with any version he constructs of statement (a). This is precisely because if it *is* a statement at all, then it must (by definition) have some content for communication, i.e. it must concern objective truth. If it has no content, then it is not a statement but a series of noises in a universe without meaning, in which even the formulation of thoughts is impossible. In such a universe, communication, if conceivable at all, would be only on a level of animal-like expressions of emotion;[1] for by the rules of statement (a) there can never be content to it. Surely therefore, none but the clinically insane could accept such a view of the universe if he really understood what it implied. Certainly any professing existentialist with whom we have talked has soon made some kind of statement, thus implicitly accepting the existence of the truth he purports to deny. To make any statement at all implies that objective truth exists.

Some, at least, of the famous people occasionally cited as holding the view in statement (a) appear in the final analysis not to do so. Jean-Paul Sartre held that neither an externally given *essence of man* nor a universal *moral code* exist, but did not deny the existence of truth. He then had a problem in giving meaning to any 'subjective' moral code, which he solved by sleight of hand and by slipping in a 'mauvaise foi' as (in effect) an external principle of the type whose existence he denied.[2] But this is not the same problem as that involved in statement (a). The existentialists may find truth (especially the essential 'thinginess' of the universe) impossible to convey, but surely do not deny its existence. Albert Camus did achieve some kind of moral detachment in *L'Etranger* (though not in *La Peste*, nor, it seems, in his own experience) but as far as we know never denied the existence of truth itself. It may well be true that certain contemporary writers have moved towards an intuitive position reflecting something like statement (a)[3] but as a cold philosophy it is totally inadequate.

Of religious existentialists, Kierkegaard may be quoted as saying: 'truth is that which makes me a better man.' We admire Kierkegaard without finding him wholly consistent. Here he seems mainly concerned that *truth* in the Danish church was cold hypothesis-proof-fact with little relevance to, or moral effect on, the church members. We observe first that his statement *is* a statement. Secondly, it even implies an external standard of 'better', a standard which would (as Sartre said) be found only in some theistic scheme of things.

A view which is related to statement (a) is sometimes held. This may be written as:
statement (b) 'All religions are saying the truth about God in their different ways.'

Now if the word 'God' has here any objective content, then one may critically examine the statement (b) in the light of what the different religions do in fact teach. The matter is then at least open to debate, and in our opinion (see section 21) the statement is false.

Alternatively the word 'God' may be redefined to mean something like 'that which you take seriously'.[4] If we do this then statement (b) is not a statement but a tautology. One might, moreover, consider with regret the confusion this creates in those for whom the word 'God' has always meant something (or someone) objective. Much of the 'new' theology which descends from Schleiermacher seems to us to be a Humpty-Dumpty-like manipulation of words in this fashion, which often turns out to consist of non-statements, and is at best misleading and emotive.

There is another view, also related to statement (a), and which may be written as:
statement (c) 'You are only saying what you say because of your upbringing.'

Now in one sense this is self-evidently true. Given a different upbringing we should quite probably not believe that the world was round, that potatoes are good to eat, that penicillin kills certain bacteria, that electricity can be used to produce light, or that Christ died for our sins. But none of these things which we believe to be fact would be any the more or any the less so, for our believing or not believing them. The best we can do is to try to recognize our biases caused by our upbringing, and decide, as rationally as we are able, what is true and what is not.

The Christian feels, for example, that the most reasonable explanations of his religious experiences are those provided by the Christian faith. Sometimes someone presents 'psychology' as a supposed alternative, smiling knowingly and saying: "You only believe it is Christ because of your upbringing—really it is all psychological." But this weapon is two-edged, for we could as well say that he only believes it is 'all psychological' because of his own upbringing! The logical conclusion of such a line of argument would be that knowledge is impossible since practically all beliefs depend on upbringing. In one sense this is true, for we are absolutely certain of nothing except perhaps our own existence. In practice, however, we do accept many 'facts' about our world, at least as working hypotheses. This does not mean that in ascertaining such facts we have a naive credulity regarding our immediate everyday impressions. We may realize only too well the mistakes made in this direction by philosophers of previous generations.[5] But to reject such naive views of the reliability of our 'experience' of our world is by no means to abandon all confidence in what we call facts. We realize today the incertitude of our knowledge, but in practice still have to accept as 'true' many working hypotheses, to serve as guides for our actions.[6] Recognizing the bias caused by our upbringing, we must still try to decide as rationally as possible what is most likely to be true, and therefore will serve best as a working hypothesis. As this book will show, there do seem to us to be good rational grounds for accepting as true the Christian hypothesis about existence and the meaning of things, and for acting accordingly. Unfortunately, however, many who say that it is 'all psychological' are not even prepared to discuss it on any such rational basis. Having told us that it is 'our upbringing' they then feel that as a matter of course the beliefs themselves must be false. Yet, strangely, they themselves continue to eat potatoes and avoid eating rat poison—also presumably as a result of beliefs acquired in their upbringing. The inconsistency of this is apparent.

When their inconsistency is pointed out, it usually transpires that they want to separate 'religious' facts from 'everyday' facts, i.e. to separate what is 'highly controversial' from what is 'universally accepted'. Now firstly we must reject any division between 'religious' facts and those of any other kind. We may indeed (see section 11) distinguish that which relates to persons from that which relates to material things, but these two categories do not correspond to 'religious' and 'non-religious' ones. During the resurrection for example, the physical disappearance of Christ's body from the tomb was certainly a 'religious' fact, and yet was also one which concerned the material world. Secondly, what 'everybody accepts' cannot seriously be defended as a criterion of truth. Whether the 'everyone' means our society or the world in general, few could accept such a criterion, and we doubt very much if it is possible to do so consistently. One may take as *part* of the evidence what everyone else believes, but one's final decision about the truth should surely be taken on the basis of the whole evidence of which this is only part.

Thus any attempt to drive a wedge between 'religious' and other knowledge is unlikely to succeed. Truths of any kind must be debated on the basis of reason and of such facts as may be accepted by both disputants. The knowledge that anyone might behave differently given a different upbringing cannot be used as a weapon by either, unless to say that knowledge of any and every kind is impossible.

We hope, therefore, that it is clear why in this book we assume that there is a single and objective truth. No human being can know it all, and language is certainly an imperfect tool to describe it, but the truth itself remains unchanged, and we must seek to know and communicate that truth better. Any other assumption about truth can only lead (as we have tried all too briefly to indicate) to contradiction or nonsense.

Further Reading:

We know of no good literature specifically on Christianity and existentialism, but there is some on related topics.

On the new theology:

Revolt Against Heaven K.Hamilton (Paternoster)
Whats New in Religion? K.Hamilton (Paternoster)
Professor Hamilton gives a scholarly, clear and penetrating analysis of the sources and ideas of the 'New Theology' and

modern religious thinking. Both books are excellent.
Set Forth Your Case Clark Pinnock (Craig)
Dr Pinnock argues that Christianity is not an irrational faith and should be presented objectively.

On philosophy:

Philosophy and the Christian Faith Colin Brown (Tyndale)
A survey of the main philosophical movements of the last 1,000 years, showing their relevance to the Christian faith. For so concise a treatment the book is remarkably clear.
The God Who is There Francis Schaeffer (Hodder)
Escape from Reason Francis Schaeffer (I.V.P.)
Dr Schaeffer outlines his views of how the objective message of Christianity is the only solution to man's problems in our modern world of relativism.

Notes for Foreword to Professing Existentialists

1. Perhaps like Beckett's *How it is*—only without a novel being possible!
2. Sartre's most concise statement of this, his early belief, was probably in *Existentialism and Humanism*.
3. *The Withered Branch* by D.S. Savage makes this point about several English writers. The book *Sartre,* by the novelist and philosopher Iris Murdoch, contains some penetrating thoughts on continental writers.
4. This is the definition in *Honest to God* p.46.
5. Descartes realized the weakness of his own suggestion that since the creator must be honest our impressions must be reliable; in practice therefore, he turned it into a statement about what we 'grasp very clearly'. Locke's *tabula rasa* concept of the mind fails to take sufficient account of the predisposition of the mind to codify its impressions in certain ways. Hume, while validly criticizing his predecessors, had in later years to admit the inadequacy of his own view of mind based on his view of ideas and perceptions. The more recent logical positivists, who regarded themselves in some ways as Hume's successors, tried to combine his scepticism of metaphysics with an optimism regarding the construction and verification of theories based on supposed 'primary experiences'; the large loopholes and inconsistencies in their approach have been demonstrated, especially by Karl Popper. This book is obviously not the place for a detailed analysis of such views, but we believe it a valid point that philosophers (especially before Kant) often did naively accept immediate impressions as indisputable.
6. This, in a slightly different way, was Hume's point, when he first really expanded the full meaning of a sceptical approach